IF IT RUNS IN YOUR FAMILY

# ARTHRITIS

## REDUCING YOUR RISK

# IF IT RUNS IN YOUR FAMILY

# ARTHRITIS

## REDUCING YOUR RISK

## Mary Dan Eades, M.D.

### Foreword by Kent Johnson, M.D.

Developed by The Philip Lief Group, Inc.

BANTAM BOOKS

NEW YORK · TORONTO · LONDON · SYDNEY · AUCKLAND

This book is not intended as a substitute for the medical advice of physicians. The reader should regularly consult a physician in matters relating to his or her health and particularly with respect to any symptoms that may require diagnosis or medical attention. Readers should also speak with their own doctors about their own individual needs before starting any diet or fitness program. Consulting one's personal physician about diet and exercise is especially important if the reader is on any medication or is already under medical care for any illness.

IF IT RUNS IN YOUR FAMILY: ARTHRITIS
A Bantam Book/February 1992

Library of Congress Cataloging-in-Publication Data
Eades, Mary Dan.
If it runs in your family : arthritis : reducing your risk / Mary
Dan Eades ; foreword by Kent Johnson.
    p.   cm.
Includes bibliographical references and index.
ISBN 0-553-35478-7
    1. Arthritis—Risk factors.   2. Arthritis—Popular works.
I. Title.
RC933.E23   1991
616.7′22—dc20                                          91-18159
                                                           CIP
Published simultaneously in the United States and Canada

Bantam Books are published by Bantam Books, a division of Bantam Doubleday
Dell Publishing Group, Inc. Its trademark, consisting of the words "Bantam Books"
and the portrayal of a rooster, is Registered in U.S. Patent and Trademark Office
and in other countries. Marca Registrada. Bantam Books, 666 Fifth Avenue, New
York, New York 10103.

PRINTED IN THE UNITED STATES OF AMERICA
OPM   0   9   8   7   6   5   4   3   2   1

For my father

# Acknowledgments

First and above all, I want to thank my father, who inspired me all my life. I wish he were here still to share this book with me. He and my mother would both have loved to have helped me with it, and I would have treasured their help.

In his absence, however, my wonderful husband and children have never failed to give me the support I needed to keep to the task, and for that and their patience, I am thankful.

And thanks to my sister, Rose Crane, for her help in accumulating so much of the lay reader material through the Arthritis Foundation and elsewhere. It was a project dear to her, too.

And finally, my thanks to my editors at Philip Lief, Alan Mahoney and Constance Jones, for their patience with the delays caused by an unexpectedly hectic clinic schedule this spring. And to Linda Loewenthal of Bantam and my friend and agent Cathy Hemming for making the project possible.

M.D.E.

# Contents

# Foreword

It is vitally important for anyone writing about the complex issues of arthritis—or for that matter on medical progress in any field—to construe the "state of the science" as accurately as possible. To accomplish this, the author must be comfortable with all the dimensions of current research that are pertinent to the disease. In cases where medical knowledge is limited, or where we have only clues—even conflicting ones—an even greater challenge arises. Contentions for which there is no scientific evidence are notoriously difficult to handle responsibly and are very susceptible to excessive posturing. All of this is particularly true in the case of arthritis.

The public of the 1990s is aggressively pursuing not only what is known about the disease but what is *not* known as well. To her credit, Dr. Eades presents a balanced view of these components and, most important, identifies scientific speculation as such whenever necessary. Her writing reflects the clinical background of a medical professional and the emotional wisdom of a patient, advocate, and friend. *If It Runs in Your Family: Arthritis* fills a crucial gap in the effort to communicate with the public about the disease. I know of no equal in the lay press addressing this topic.

The book is written in a lucid, informal style that makes the scientific aspects of the topics she covers easy to digest. As a clinician, I can attest that this is no easy feat, particularly when the issues invoke research into the frontiers of immunogenetics— the study of genetic influences on immunological disorders. The chapter explaining the genetic predilection for some forms of arthritis reflects the best of Dr. Eades's impressive diagnostic skills as a doctor and her ability to bring the emotional aspects of medical care into unique and sympathetic perspective. She defines arthritis and related diseases and describes their diagnosis and treatment with simplicity and precision.

Throughout the book the role of the patient in determining the course of the battle that is to be waged against arthritis is emphasized. The most important questions that come up for anyone facing the disease are

- What can one do to minimize his or her risk for the disease, with or without a family history?
- Is the expression of the inheritance element in any way under the control of the individual?

In addressing these issues Dr. Eades deals with lifestyle decisions and addresses general health measures such as diet, exercise, and stress. On the one hand, the exact role these factors play in affecting the triggering of disease is not known, and their effect on the expression of existing disease is, in general, poorly understood. On the other, as human beings we like to think that, despite inheriting a predisposition, it is in our power to control its expression, at least to a degree. Dr. Eades's belief in the human spirit supports this power.

Throughout, the author thoughtfully probes these matters

with an eye toward distinguishing what is scientifically established from what is speculative. Her important achievement is accomplishing the goal of effectively and realistically communicating with the public about these issues, and I hope accordingly that her book will receive a wide audience among patients and the public at large.

KENT R. JOHNSON, M.D.
Bethesda, Maryland

# 1

# At Risk for Arthritis

## A Personal Perspective

I awoke this morning aware of the nagging stiffness in my hands. Some mornings, and today is one of those, the ache will center more persistently in one joint—the culprit this time is the third finger of my left hand. The pain is not severe, in fact, it rarely prompts me to take so much as an aspirin or over-the-counter ibuprofen tablet, and it's usually gone by the time I've had a cup of coffee and limbered my hands a bit packing lunches and getting breakfast together for the kids. So what's the big deal? At thirty-something don't we all have a few aches and pains and a little stiffness in the morning? Sure. But from the deepest recesses of my mind, a soft whisper cautions: Are you sure it's thirty-something stiffness or could it be something more? The doubt hovers at the edges of my consciousness because I am one of the legion of Americans at risk for arthritis.

For me and millions like me for whom the specter of arthritic crippling looms large from the roots of our family trees, it could always be something more. We don't dwell on the possibility, but with each insistent ache in a finger, an unusual stiffness in the wrist or knee, a nagging pain in the lower back comes that cautionary whisper: Do I have it, too?

I have heard the murmurings of that whisper since my early teen years, when I first recognized that the disease that was relentlessly crippling my father was something I could inherit. He recognized this possibility, too, and I think that the knowledge that arthritis might one day strike one of his children worried my father more than his dread of what the disease could do to him.

At that time, he had no hard medical data about what prompted a person to develop arthritis, but he formulated his own theories. For example, he believed that stress and body overuse and abuse had contributed to his disease, which created quite a dilemma. On the one hand, my father was a man who always gave 100 percent, went the extra mile, accepted the short end of any stick with grace, and expected those around him to strive for excellence, too. He taught us never to accept from ourselves less than our very best. On the other hand, he was a man determined not to see his children succumb to a crippling disease that he felt was strongly connected to stress; he constantly implored us not to worry, not to push too hard, not to overtax ourselves. It makes for an interesting juggling act always to strive for excellence while not overtaxing yourself.

And so despite his warnings (and truly with his support and blessing), I chose a path that many would consider fraught with worry and stress and one that required me many times—especially during my training years—to challenge my limits of physical and mental endurance. I became a physician. In the subsequent years, my training and research into the subject of arthritis have led me to believe that my father's theory about stress as one of the promoters of the disease is not without medical validity; he knew this without years of training and without ever having read a single research article on the subject, because he had lived it firsthand.

He first developed the symptoms of rheumatoid arthritis during his senior year in college. He was just short of forty, having abandoned a successful plumbing business to pursue the dream of a college education. He, at thirty-five, and my mother sold their home and headed off to college with a brood of children and what they hoped were enough savings to see us through. As is so often the case, the money ran out sooner than expected, and my father had to interrupt his college dream for a year to return to work full-time. Consequently, my mother finished her training ahead of him and returned home to take a job teaching English at our local high school.

My father still had thirty hours of course work ahead of him to finish his civil engineering degree. He faced two full college semesters and a school year's separation from his family, which he could not accept. As was usually the case with my father, he believed that anything he put his mind to was possible, and so he decided he could take the full load in a single semester, while still making an eight-hour commute each weekend to visit us. And he did. He came to feel in later years, however, that the price he paid may have been too high. It was during that grueling semester that he suffered the first attack of arthritis in his feet.

Whether the development of his disease at this time occurred coincidental to the stress of this impossible situation or whether the stress really contributed to the development of arthritis in an already genetically susceptible individual, we may never know. But that semester marked the beginning of my father's twenty-year battle with rheumatoid arthritis. His was one of the most virulent cases I have ever witnessed, and although I must concede that the disease crippled and consumed him physically, I can say that it never conquered his spirit. When he died in 1983 of heart disease, he was one joint replacement away from walking again.

Those of us who have witnessed firsthand the ravages of the severely crippling forms of arthritis in a family member have a deep and visceral understanding of what it means to be at risk for arthritis. We share a fear that we keep carefully tucked away in the backs of our minds that perhaps a fight against arthritis may await us in the future. After all, we know that arthritis runs in the family, don't we?

I can say with certainty, both as a physician and as a person at risk, that we can and do inherit a *susceptibility* to develop arthritic diseases of several kinds: rheumatoid arthritis, gouty arthritis, osteoarthritis, the spondylopathies (the spine-fusing arthritic conditions, or arthritides, that include ankylosing spondylitis, psoriatic arthritis, and Reiter's syndrome), and many other rarer forms. But does inheriting a susceptibility mean we will actually develop the disease? No. In the case of the arthritides, a genetic predisposition does not a disease make. The inherited genetic message requires an environmental catalyst to set the wheels of arthritic disease into motion. But how and when did this inherited message gain entry into the genes of humankind?

Our medical understanding of the causes and methods of inheritance of the various forms of arthritis has exploded during the last several decades, in large measure because of some fairly recent technologic advances in the fields of immune and molecular biology. These advances would not have been possible, however, without the groundwork laid by centuries of inquiry into a disease that has baffled, confounded, and intrigued medical scientists and researchers for thousands of years. And so, let me begin to answer this question of how we inherit arthritis by first turning back the clock to look at its place in our history.

## From the Viewpoint of History

As long as man has existed, so has some form of arthritis. We see traces of arthritic deformity in the unearthed bones of our earliest *Homo* ancestors of 2 million years ago. X-ray studies of bones from the mummies of ancient Egypt attest that these people, too, suffered from arthritis. The skeletal record tells us that as the history of man marched forward, so did arthritic disease.

The early physicians of Greece and Rome were the first to make a written record of the occurrence of arthritis among their patients. They not only named many of the diseases (we use many of the names in modified form today), but left beautifully detailed descriptions of the symptoms and their treatments. Some of the "cures" would seem bizarre to us in a modern medical context, but others retain medical validity even now. For example, just as modern physicians prescribe heat and hot water therapy for their arthritic patients, so did the physicians of ancient Rome. The Roman populace apparently suffered arthritis to such a great degree—some sources placing the figure at more than 70 percent of the over-thirty population affected by some form of arthritis—that historians believe one of the chief functions of the Roman bath may have been therapeutic, i.e., to ease the aching, painful joints of a substantial segment of the people. Other remedies ranged from avoidance of mead and fortified wines (measures still in use to combat frequent attacks of gout) to diuretics and purges and even to electrical stimulation therapy, in which the patients shocked their arthritic feet by placing them on "electric" eels and fish. This latter method may have benefited the patients in a manner similar to our modern use of *TENS* (transcutaneous electrical nerve stimulator) therapy: controlling pain by passing low-level electrical current across the affected area.

Gout, another of the inherited arthritic diseases, was first described quite accurately by Hippocrates in the fourth century B.C., and even then it was considered a disease of dietary excess. By the fourteenth and fifteenth centuries it had become a disease of affluence. Only those people rich enough to afford a daily diet rich in calories, heavy meats, exotic seafoods, aged cheeses, and fortified wines could develop gout. And so we think of gouty arthritis during this period of history as a disease of nobles and aristocrats. We see them in the portraits of the day, furs and jewels draping their rotund bellies, dour expressions perhaps betraying the pain of standing on a gouty toe.

If gout was a disease of dietary excesses, then did the starving masses escape unscathed? From gout, probably yes. From arthritis? Hardly. The first widespread outbreak in Europe of another, perhaps even more fearsome form of inherited crippling arthritis—rheumatoid arthritis—occurred chiefly among the poorer masses during the time of the industrial revolution. Lack of proper sanitation; overcrowding, which leads to rampant infectious disease; and inadequate nutrition probably all played roles in the development of epidemic numbers of cases of rheumatoid arthritis among the wretched and downtrodden population. In chapter 3, we will examine the roles of stress, infection, and nutrition as contributors to the development of the inherited arthritides in detail, but for now, suffice it to say that underlying poor health and chronic malnutrition may have served to open the lid of Pandora's proverbial box in regard to rheumatoid arthritis during this era.

Perhaps at no time in history can we more clearly implicate the effects of environment in promoting an arthritis as in early nineteenth-century Europe. However, we cannot hold the environmental factors solely to blame; the genetic messages necessary to develop the disease had to already be present in the European bloodlines. How long had they been there? Who can say. The best answer is from the moment that the first of their ancestors acquired the genetic message that would, under the proper stimulation, express itself in the development of that particular form of arthritis. We know with certainty, however, that the disease existed in Europe as much as two centuries earlier, attested to not by a written record but by an oil pigment one. We can recognize the joint deformities typical of rheumatoid arthritis in subjects painted by Peter Paul Rubens during the seventeenth century.

And so throughout history, arthritic diseases have afflicted humans and have baffled, confounded, and fascinated healers and scientists. Modern medical researchers continue to search for clues to the causes and cures for arthritis. However, they often meet with frustration and difficulty, because arthritis is not a single disease, but a cluster of diseases with a common end point: inflammation and, all too frequently, destruction and deformity of the joints. Although the end point for all these diseases is the same, they may affect widely different areas of the body besides the joints, may be inherited by different mechanisms, and may respond differently to various remedies. You may already be familiar with the major forms of arthritic disease—the ones I alluded to previously—rheumatoid arthritis, osteoarthritis, gouty arthritis, the spondylopathies, and systemic lupus; however, for the sake of clarity for readers who may not know these terms, let me take a moment to discuss each one of them.

## The Major Forms of Inherited Arthritis

I have elected—keeping in mind the available space and reasonable scope of this book—to cover the five broad categories of inherited arthritis that I believe will encompass the vast majority of Americans. I would be remiss, however, were I not to make you aware that researchers in this area have identified more than 100 separate types of arthritis. Many of the diseases are quite rare and some of them appear to have no inherited pattern; therefore, they have no specific place in a book devoted to diseases that run in the family. For readers who have a special interest in learning more about these other forms of arthritis, I recommend contacting your local chapter of the Arthritis Foundation. I have listed the addresses for these chapters in chapter 9. This first-rate national organization maintains high-quality, up-to-date educational and self-help materials that they provide inexpensively—or in most cases free of charge—to arthritis sufferers, their families, and any other interested parties. One of the major goals of the Arthritis Foundation is education. Contact them; they will be pleased to help you in any way they can to understand and cope with any of the 100 arthritic diseases.

In chapter 2, you will begin to trace the occurrence of arthritis in your family. To make sense of what your risk for a specific kind of arthritic disease may be, however, you will naturally need to know what kinds of arthritis have developed in your family members. In many cases, it may not be possible to know which particular type of joint disease afflicted your aunts, uncles, grandparents, and even parents and siblings, but you will find the task easier if I provide you with a thumbnail sketch of the classic features of each of the major arthritides. With this information, you will be able to at least make a reasonably educated guess about which type of arthritis has affected members in your family, even though you may not be certain.

## Rheumatoid Arthritis

Permit me to begin with this form of inherited arthritis, which occurs in about 1 out of every 100 Americans—currently its victims number about 7 million in the United States. Although rheumatoid arthritis (RA) is certainly not the most common form of arthritis—that designation belongs to osteoarthritis, which affects 1 in 14 Americans—it is the disease that crippled my father, and is, therefore, of particular interest to me. This form of inherited arthritis is two to three times more common in women than men and usually begins between ages forty and sixty, but it can strike at any time, even in childhood. It affects all racial and ethnic groups.

RA is a chronic inflammatory and frequently destructive and deforming disease of the joints, but its effects may be more widespread in the body, sometimes progressing to involve the arteries, nerves, eyes, pericardium (lining over the heart), lymph glands, and spleen. The degree to which a person will be afflicted with this or any arthritic disease can vary markedly even within a single family. Some people may be severely affected—such as my father was—exhibiting virtually every possible complication of RA, whereas in others the disease may be so mild as to escape diagnosis. Even cases of *spontaneous remission* (all aspects of the disease resolving mysteriously) do occasionally occur. How or why this happens, researchers have yet to ascertain. It only appears that in these miracle cases of remission, the immune system "turns off" the exaggerated response that had previously "turned on." Let me back up and explain how.

Genetic messages involving the immune system are contained in the chromosomes (the genes) and are passed from parent to child to create a susceptibility for RA. However, the development of the disease occurs in response to certain triggers such as infection, malnutrition, and stress, which we will discuss in greater detail in chapters 2 and 3. This triggering stimulus activates the inflammatory pathways in the susceptible immune system in a manner similar to tipping the first of a series of carefully positioned dominoes—one component of the inflammatory reaction trips the next and the next and so on, but in an exaggerated fashion, which may not respond to the body's "normal" signals to stop the process.

The series of reactions first causes the lining of the joint cavity—the *synovium* or *synovial membrane*—to swell and then to undergo hypertrophy or grow, increasing both the number and the size of the lining cells (see below). The swollen, actively growing lining—called *pannus*—that now protrudes into the joint cavity, contains many inflammatory blood cells (which nor-

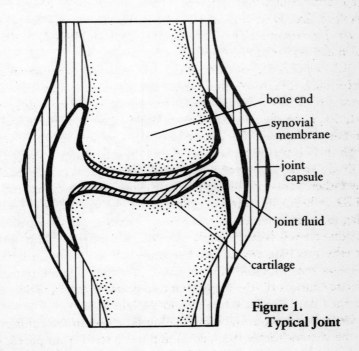

bone end

synovial membrane

joint capsule

joint fluid

cartilage

**Figure 1.
Typical Joint**

mally function to protect us from invasion by viruses and bacteria). These inflammatory cells produce substances (enzymes) that digest and destroy the structural framework of the smooth cartilage covering the ends of the bones and the soft tissues—ligaments and tendons—that support and surround the joint. Over time, the damaged ends of the bones may fuse together either with a bridge of fibrous tissue or even with solid bony tissue, resulting in joint deformity and crippling.

It is, however, the enzyme warfare waged on the joint by the digestive substances that results in the classic symptoms of joint inflammation seen in patients with RA: redness, warmth, a spongy or mushy swelling, stiffness, and often severe pain of the affected joints. The onset of symptoms may be gradual over several weeks or months, or may—in perhaps 20 percent of cases—erupt dramatically over the space of only a few days. Early symptoms may include fatigue and malaise (a sense of discomfort, uneasiness, or the loss of the feeling of well-being, which occurs in virtually any disease state), low-grade fever, weight loss, and depression. A whole host of early symptoms may presage the development of RA, and I will discuss these symptoms and the tools of diagnosis more fully in chapter 4, but let's first look for a moment—because all arthritic diseases do not favor the same pattern of joints—at which joints RA usually affects. (Note: the pattern of joints involved is an important differentiating clue in your identification of "unknown" types of arthritic disease in various family members, and so you should pay particular attention to information you discover about which joints are affected in your search of your family's medical history.)

Rheumatoid arthritis tends to strike joints in a paired fashion, i.e., both wrists, both knees. Classically, it is the hands, wrists, knees, and feet that suffer most often—but any *diarthrodal* (hinge-type) joint can be affected. Involvement of the spine usually occurs only in the neck and spares the middle and lower regions of the back. The wrists almost without fail will be affected. In the hands, RA almost never involves the joints at the ends of the fingers, but instead seems to concentrate on the middle finger joints and the knuckle joints (medically termed the MCP, standing for metacarpal-phalangeal) where the finger meets the hand. When these particular joints become unstable with progression of the disease process, the mechanical pull of the muscles and tendons on them results in the typical appearance of the crippled rheumatoid hand: the wrists often are quite swollen; the fingers, deformed and swollen at the middle joints and most prominently at the MCP joints, deviate away from the thumb and toward the side of the little finger. (This pattern of deformity of the hand is what we recognize as RA in the seventeenth-century Rubens paintings.) A quite similar process occurs in the feet as well, with the ankles swollen and the toes "pulling" to the sides.

Please do not despair that if you discover this kind of arthritis lurking in your family tree you are doomed to develop such deformities. Even if you should develop active rheumatoid arthritis, with early expert intervention now available in the medical community, you can prevent most of these crippling deformities; we will examine how in chapters 4 and 5. For this disease as with all arthritis, the name of the game is *prevention:* prevention of development, if possible, and, should the disease develop, prevention of crippling through early diagnosis and treatment.

### Osteoarthritis

Here, we confront the most common of all arthritides, with some sources alleging it to be universally present to varying degrees in all people more than sixty-five years of age. Current estimates by the Arthritis Foundation put the number of people afflicted with osteoarthritis—in the United States alone—at 16 million. I would wager that there are few Americans who do not have an older relative or two with at least a minor degree of osteoarthritis. Researchers have long theorized that the chief mechanism behind the pervasiveness of this form of arthritis is simply years of use. If that is the case, then osteoarthritis becomes nothing more than the end result of a lifetime of chronic daily stresses on joints, which eventually wear down—or even wear out—their smooth cartilage surfaces, leaving them creaking, stiff, painful, and arthritic.

Certainly, daily wear and tear of joints plays a critical role in the development of this form of arthritic disease, but it now appears that it may not be the sole culprit. For example, if we accept a theory of repetitive trauma as the single causative factor in osteoarthritis, we would expect to see a greater incidence of arthritis in the right hands of right-handed people—because this hand receives more daily use—which, in fact, we do. But by the same token, we would also expect to see an increase in arthritis in the knees of those marathon runners who continue to run high numbers of miles well into advanced age, and (at least in men) we do not. Nor do we seem to see an increase in arthritis of the hands, wrists, and shoulders of jackhammer operators, and who could argue that these joints receive an incredible amount of daily repetitive trauma. Although no one could reasonably dispute a place for chronic wear and tear in the development of osteoarthritis, the results of medical studies into the role of prolonged occupational or sports stresses have been inconsistent. It would appear, therefore, that we must attribute the development of osteoarthritis to more than simply the wearing out of joints.

Could it be that, as in the case of other arthritic diseases, the impact of environment must be superimposed on a susceptible genetic framework? Research tells us that indeed this is probably so: that, except in the severest cases of traumatic joint destruction (and by that, I mean serious joint fractures and dislocations such as would occur in major moving-vehicle crashes, serious sports injuries, and the like) in which osteoarthritic changes develop virtually without exception, the day-to-day trauma to joints only serves to stimulate the development of arthritis in those persons with an inherited predisposition for it. We will be exploring the roles of inheritance and environment in contributing to arthritis more fully in the next two chapters, and so for the moment, let me simply introduce you to the disease itself.

Most readers will recognize the pattern of swollen joints and symptoms typical of osteoarthritis from having seen the disease firsthand among older relatives and friends. Especially—but not exclusively—in older women, the disease attacks the small joints of the hands, in particular, those closest to the ends of the fingertips, medically termed the DIP joints. The name DIP stands for *distal* (meaning farthest from the center of the body), *inter-* (meaning between), and *phalangeal* (the individual bones of the finger or toe). Aside from these joints, the PIP (proximal—i.e., nearest—interphalangeal) joint, which is the middle knuckle of the fingers, the weight-bearing joints (knees and hips), and the spine (mainly the neck and lower back) appear to suffer most often.

Perhaps your grandmother or great-grandmother had the knobby deformities of her finger joints that we call Heberden's (or Bouchard's) nodes. These "knobs" are actually bony growths, or bone spurs, that arise near the joint and deform it. They are typical of the osteoarthritic process as it occurs in joints throughout the body, but nowhere more visibly than in the hands. What happens to cause these deformities?

One plausible theory suggests that the process is set into motion by some instigating event (chronic trauma to the joint surface, perhaps) that leads to the release of chemicals (enzymes) that, in turn, begin to digest the framework of the cartilage. Under normal circumstances, this enzyme release would serve a remodeling or rehabilitating function, i.e., to digest damaged cartilage cells, remove the debris, and allow repair with new healthy cells.

As the cartilage ages, however, the normal repair cycle begins to fail. The surface of the joint becomes stiffer, less flexible, and less able to serve as a resilient shock absorber—in short, more susceptible to damage from lesser and lesser amounts of stress. As the wear-and-tear process continues and the ability to repair the daily damage falls ever farther behind the rate of wearing down, large portions—or in some cases even all—of the cartilage covering of the bone end may ultimately wear away. The result, which appears gradually over years, is the grating stiffness and painful, swollen, creaking joints of osteoarthritis.

To compound the insult of the body's no longer being able to maintain a healthy repaired joint surface, recent studies suggest that substances released by the exposed and damaged cartilage and bone cells may also incite the body's immune system. Once activated, the immune system sets off the same sort of domino effect that I described for rheumatoid arthritis, leading to inflammation of the arthritic joint, with worsening of pain and further decreased mobility.

### Gouty Arthritis

Although physicians since the time of Hippocrates have held that dietary excesses and indiscretions promote the development of gouty arthritis, they have also over the intervening 2,000 years of medical history recognized its strong tendency to run in families. And so we find once again, the critical interplay of environment (in this case what we eat) with our genetic heritage.

Nowadays—especially in the United States—the masses of people, far from starving, consume a diet rich in sugars, fatty meats, and alcohol. No longer is dietary excess the province of the privileged classes, of those at the pinnacle of affluence. With year-round and seemingly limitless availability of high-calorie (and sadly, often low-nutrition) foods in the American supermarkets and fast-food chains, we have become a nation of "dietary aristocrats," many of whom will fall victim to that commonest form of inflammatory joint disease in men over the age of thirty—gout. I should point out, however, that although gout does occur most commonly among middle-aged men, women past menopause also suffer from this form of arthritis.

In fact, the Arthritis Foundation currently estimates that nearly 2 million Americans suffer from attacks of gout. Although you have all most likely heard of gout and may have relatives who have suffered from attacks of it, you may not know precisely what it *is* or understand how what you eat could cause arthritis. Let's look at the disease.

A single basic chemical overabundance is at work in the development of gout: a substance called *uric acid*. In humans, this chemical is the end point of the digestion of proteins. Under normal circumstances, our bodies excrete the uric acid as waste from the kidneys. However, about 90 percent of patients afflicted with gout, for various reasons, fail to do so adequately, resulting in abnormally high levels of uric acid in their blood and in certain body tissues—including the fluid in their joints. As of yet, researchers have not identified one particular genetic defect that causes this group of people to *undersecrete*—or retain—uric acid, but the search continues. In another group—constituting perhaps 10 percent of gout sufferers—genetic specialists have identified the lack of a specific enzyme passed along from parent to child on the X chromosome, which leads to gout because of *overproduction* of uric acid, not a failure to eliminate enough of it. Again, let me save a more in-depth examination of the genetic bases of these diseases for chapter 2 and turn to a description of the classic picture of gout to assist you in your identification of family members' arthritides.

Far and away the most common joint to be involved in gouty arthritic attacks is the one that joins the great toe to the foot—medically called the first metatarsophalangeal joint (MTP). Affliction of this joint has been termed *podagra,* which I recall being told in medical school roughly translates to "foot caught in a trap." I have made mention of this translation through my years of medical practice to patients—usually portly middle-aged men—who limp painfully into the examination room and expose for my viewing a red, hot, swollen, exquisitely tender great toe joint. These men uniformly give me a slightly pained smile and knowing nod and probably wish I would cut the history lesson short and do something for their extreme discomfort. Still in the end, they uniformly agree that the description fits and that whoever came up with such an apt name must surely have personally suffered the disease.

The unenviable pain and sudden onset of a gouty attack has never been more eloquently described than by Sir Thomas Sydenham, a British physician of the seventeenth century, who wrote,

The victim goes to bed and sleeps in good health. About two o'clock in the morning he is awakened by a severe pain in the great toe; more rarely in the heel, ankle, or instep. This pain is like that of a dislocation, and yet the parts feel as if cold water were poured over them. . . . So exquisite and lively meanwhile is the feeling of the part affected that it cannot bear the weight of the bedclothes nor the jar of a person walking in the room.*

Indeed, in three-fourths of patients, the first attack will begin in just such a fashion, abruptly and in the middle of the night. Often the attack follows a binge of eating and drinking, an injury, or occasionally physical stress (such as other illness or an operation). What happens to cause such excruciating pain?

As I have said, the underlying problem is that gout sufferers have too much uric acid circulating in their blood and the fluid surrounding their joints, as a result of either making too much of the acid or not getting rid of enough of it through the kidneys. If the level of this chemical is already high, and someone then binges on foods and drinks likely to send it abruptly skyrocketing, a concentration of uric acid may develop that is so high it can no longer remain suspended in the body's fluids and so precipitates out as a solid crystal. This process is analagous to filling a glass with warm water and shaking salt into it. If you stir the salty water, you can continue to mix in salt and it dissolves in the water—up to a point. After that, if you continue to add salt, you will ultimately exceed the amount that the water can hold, and the excess will remain as crystals on the bottom of the glass. A chemist would say you had *supersaturated* the saltwater solution. The same phenomenon occurs with the uric acid and gout: a point of supersaturation occurs and crystals of sodium urate (the "salt" of uric acid) begin to form in the joint fluid and certain other body tissues and organs, such as the kidneys (promoting the development of kidney stones, another very painful consequence of elevated uric acid).

In the joints, the crystals incite a vigorous inflammatory re-

*R. Shumacher, J. Klippel, and D. Robinson, eds., *Primer on Rheumatic Diseases,* 9th edition, Altanta: Arthritis Foundation, 1988, p. 199.

action—the crystals become the stimulus that tips the first domino—and suddenly the cardinal signs of inflammation ensue: redness, warmth, swelling, and, in this case, extreme pain. And *voilà,* the foot is caught in a trap.

In most cases, the early attacks usually stop after about a week, even if untreated, leaving a normal-appearing and pain-free joint. (Let me add that appropriate medical therapy can lead to resolution of the painful symptoms much more quickly.) With the passage of time, however, without medical and/or dietary intervention to reduce the level of uric acid in the blood, another attack will surely occur. As the disease progresses, the "normal" pain-free interval between acute attacks grows shorter, the duration of the attacks grows longer, and, usually, the disease begins to affect other joints as well. Left untreated, the ongoing inflammation can erode the cartilage surface and the underlying bone of the joints and lead to deformity and crippling, just as in RA and osteoarthritis.

In gout, however—more so than in any other arthritic disease—early diagnosis, careful adherence to dietary guidelines, and, if necessary, medication to lower uric acid levels can control the disease and absolutely prevent painful attacks and the crippling of chronic, untreated gouty arthritis. We will examine precisely how in subsequent chapters.

### The Spondylopathies

I have grouped under this category four separate arthritic conditions that differ in many ways, but that share a common joint feature: some degree of bony fusion of the spine. The name derives from the Greek *spondylos,* meaning "vertebra," one of the bones of the spine.

Hereditary factors play a strong role in all the spondylopathies, but again, what is passed on is only a *susceptibility,* which requires some sort of infectious or other environmental catalyst to initiate the development of disease. The joint disease that develops differs from osteoarthritis, rheumatoid arthritis, and gout in that the major site of inflammation occurs not only in the synovial membrane (joint lining) but at the spot where the ligaments attach onto the bones.

In the spine, each vertebra attaches to its neighbors above and below and to the cushioning disks between them by tough ligaments on all sides. The inflammatory changes that cause pain and stiffness in the attachment sites in these ligaments (and in ligaments elsewhere in the body) also incite a process of repair by laying down new bone; the "repair" causes the problems, because it goes too far. Ultimately, the inflamed ligaments completely ossify, which means that specialized bone-forming (bone-repairing) cells deposit calcium and phosphorous and other mineral salts within them and, quite literally, transform them to bone. When this occurs in a hip joint or a finger joint, the joint becomes "frozen" or fixed in one position. The same process occurs in the ligaments that join the vertebrae, leaving the normally freely flexible joints of the spine rigidly fixed.

The spondylopathies differ in degree, in location, in their predilection for involving other joints (hips, knees, feet, hands, etc.), and in the effects the disease has on other parts of the body outside the musculoskeletal framework (the eyes, skin, intestinal tract, heart, etc.).

Although they share a single inherited immune-system marker—the HLA-B27 antigen about which you will learn in the next chapter—they appear to have different environmental triggers that prompt development of the arthritis. Medical research has documented a case for infection with certain bacteria as the triggering stimulus for all the spondylopathies, but none more clearly than Reiter's syndrome.

Although the arthritis seen in these four diseases will appear much the same, let's take each of the spondylopathies in its turn and examine the features that will help to identify it.

*Ankylosing Spondylitis (Fusing Spinal Arthritis).* Although you may not have known what to call it, many of you will have seen people afflicted with ankylosing spondylitis (AS). Its victims are most often men, and its deformity is quite easy to recognize when fully developed, even to the untrained eye. In its fullest expression and most debilitating form, this arthritis leaves its victim's spine bent like an archer's bow from neck to low back; in severe cases, hips and knees may also become involved. Thus medical intervention early on is absolutely necessary.

In part to ease the strain on these joints, but also to compensate for the spinal curve, the patient with AS may develop an even more exaggerated posture, bending slightly at the hips and knees and stooping forward. This posture, however, worsens the bowing deformity of the spine even more and may ultimately cause the spine to fuse solidly in the awkwardly stooped position.

Fortunately, nowadays most patients are not fully crippled by AS, even when the whole spine, from neck to tailbone, is involved. Also, many patients—women in particular—may develop the disease only in the pelvic joints and the lower back or may even escape involvement of the spine all together. In about 25 to 30 percent of cases of AS, the joints of the limbs—especially the legs and feet—will eventually develop some degree of arthritis.

Because of the insidious nature of AS and its crippling potential in those who do develop it, the watchword is *prevention*—true for all forms of inherited arthritis, but perhaps even more important with AS. Those people in families who are at higher risk for AS must have a clear understanding of its early symptoms. Knowing what to look for will prompt earlier medical consultation and diagnosis when the symptoms first appear, at a stage when scrupulous adherence to proper posture, exercise, and medical therapeutic recommendations can maintain a functional, straight spine. I have devoted space in later chapters to not only the genetic and environmental causes of AS but also to the early symptoms, diagnosis, and therapies to prevent disability from it.

*Psoriatic Arthritis.*   Television acquainted the nation with the skin manifestation of this disease in advertisements touting remedies for "the heartbreak of psoriasis." The phrase became a part of pop culture, appearing in cartoons, comedy skits, and sitcoms. The bare truth of the matter, however, is that about 5 to 7 percent of patients suffering from psoriasis will not only develop the chronic, scaling skin condition but an arthritis of the spine and other joints as well.

The pattern of joint involvement—our usual ally in differentiating the arthritides—doesn't give us as much help in this case, because the joints affected can vary quite a bit in psoriatic arthritis. About 95 percent of the time, a combination of spinal and peripheral joints (all but the spine, pelvis, and shoulder girdle) occurs. However, that leaves a small group of about 5 percent in which only the spine is involved, making for some confusion between this form of arthritis and AS.

You can look for two major features to help you differentiate between these two forms of spinal arthritis in your family members. The first is a rash; at some point in the course of the disease there will *always* be the classic eczema or skin rash in patients with psoriatic arthritis. In the typical case, a thick scablike scale with a silvery white sheen to it usually forms on the scalp, elbows, and knees, but can occur on virtually any area of the skin.

The second clue comes from the nails and tissues around them, which will usually show one or more of the following changes: discoloration; pitting (scattered round dents that deform the smooth nail surface); fragmentation (splitting or peeling); and onycholysis (pronounced ahn-nee-ko-LIE-sis), which is a (usually) painful separation of the nail from its bed of tissue. The separation typically occurs at the tip of the nail and will leave the normal smooth curve of the "white" at the end of the nail jagged and dipping farther than normal down into the "quick."

The ends of the fingers from the last joint out (the DIP) will usually swell and take on a clublike shape, and the entirety of the finger may swell, giving it a sausagelike appearance. This characteristic—the so-called sausage digit—also occurs in the related arthritic condition of Reiter's syndrome, which we will discuss next.

Some researchers believe the environmental trigger in psoriatic arthritis to be bacterial, in particular the *Streptococcus* (which you may be familiar with as the cause of strep throat and scarlet fever). We will explore this and other possibilities, such as trauma, in greater detail in a later chapter. But whatever the trigger—be it infectious or traumatic—in those people who carry the genetic susceptibility, a domino cascade such as we have discussed in rheumatoid arthritis ensues, and the arthritis develops. The destructive inflammatory process involves not only the joints themselves but the bony covering or periosteum, the tendons, and the attachment site of the ligaments and tendons.

*Reiter's Syndrome.* In the early part of the twentieth century, Hans Reiter, a German physician, described an illness characterized by three specific symptoms: arthritis, conjunctivitis (infection or inflammation of the clear filmy covering over the eye), and urethritis (infection of the urine passageway from the bladder to the outside). During that era, the observed occurrence of this particular kind of usually venereally passed urinary-tract infection, with the subsequent development of arthritis, added yet another dimension to the picture of arthritis as a disease of excesses: gluttony, alcoholism, and now venery or sexual promiscuity.

Because the existing mores and sexual taboos of the early part of the twentieth century resulted in an overwhelming preponderance of cases of urinary infections of a venereal nature in men, the prevailing medical belief at the time was that Reiter's syndrome was a disease exclusive to men. In fact, as recently as the late 1970s, most medical texts still described the syndrome as occurring virtually only in men. It has only been within the last decade that medical scientists have recognized that in women the instigating infection can be a cystitis (bladder infection) or a cervicitis (an infection of the uterine cervix). In many cases, these kinds of infections in women may cause few symptoms and, therefore, go undetected. For this reason, physicians for years may have attributed arthritis related to Reiter's syndrome to other causes in women. In subsequent years, research has confirmed a number of infectious triggers for Reiter's syndrome, but as we have seen for the other forms of inherited arthritis, infection is but a stimulus to the development of disease in those who carry genes that make them susceptible to it.

In tracing the disease in your family, look for these typical features that will aid your identification. The arthritis usually appears two to six weeks after the onset of an infection of the urinary tract (often a cystitis, urethritis, or cervicitis); about half of those affected also have the conjunctivitis, or eye infection; the arthritis usually does not strike both joints of a pair; and, finally, the knees and ankles are the joints most commonly involved. Four other telltale signs that may help to confirm that a case of arthritis is indeed Reiter's syndrome are general swelling of at least one entire finger or toe (the sausage digits seen also in psoriatic arthritis), swelling or tenderness in the Achilles tendon (the large thick tendon from the calf muscles that attaches on the back of the ankle at the top of the heel bone), tenderness of the front end of the heel bone on the sole of the foot, and, finally, lower back pain from inflammation of the pelvic joints and the lower part of the spine.

*Enteropathic Spondylopathies (Ulcerative Colitis and Crohn's Disease).* These inherited arthritides occur together with the two major inflammatory diseases of the bowels, ulcerative colitis and Crohn's disease. For the most part, the arthritis suffered by people who develop these intestinal diseases takes a backseat to their bowel symptoms, and so for clarity's sake let me briefly describe the two syndromes for you. If you have had a family member afflicted with either of these disorders, you will likely recognize the symptoms.

Ulcerative colitis—as its name implies—usually only involves the colon or large intestine and rectum. The inflammation causes ulcers or erosions to form on the lining layer (or mucosa) of the large intestine. The patient usually suffers bouts of bloody diarrhea and painful spasm interspersed with periods of relatively normal bowel habits.

In Crohn's disease (also called regional enteritis), the inflammation causes ulcers that damage the entire wall of the bowel, affecting the lining layer, the middle muscular layer, and the outer covering layer. It occurs most often in the colon and the last portion of the small intestine, but instead of confining itself only to the colon, Crohn's disease can attack any portion of the bowel from the stomach on down. Because the erosions involve the whole of the wall of the bowel, abdominal abscesses occur much more frequently in this form of inflammatory bowel disease, and as a consequence, people who suffer it may have had multiple operations to remove diseased portions of the bowel.

The pattern and kind of joint symptoms that accompany these bowel diseases are similar, and so for our purposes here, differentiating between the two is not of critical importance to you in determining family risk.

A peripheral arthritis (one not involving the spine or pelvis) develops in perhaps 15 to 20 percent of patients with these intestinal disorders, and although it can cause crippling deformity, it is very often a temporary, nondestructive (not crippling or deforming) one. The painful swelling may migrate from joint to joint—that is, it may trouble a knee for a few days then subside there and move on to an ankle or a wrist. It may strike any joint, but of the peripheral joints, it seems to affect the knees and ankles most often.

Because I have grouped these arthritides among the spondylopathies, you will have already guessed that they, too, will involve the spine. In fact, 20 percent of patients with these inflammatory intestinal problems will have arthritis in the pelvic joints (specifically, the sacroiliac, or SI, joints) and 4 or 5 percent of them will have frank ankylosis, or fusion, of the vertebral bones along some parts of the spine. About half of these people carry the same genetic marker—the HLA-B27 antigen—that we associate with AS, and although the bowel-related arthritis is usually less severe, the bony changes it causes in the spine are identical to those found in AS.

To identify family members who may have suffered this kind of arthritis, look for primarily knee, ankle, and spinal problems associated with chronic (long-standing) bowel problems that may have required the intermittent use of special medications to control their symptoms and often hospital stays for severe flare-ups or operations on the bowel.

### Systemic Lupus Erythematosus

Although this disease—which I will refer to as SLE for the sake of expediency—will often involve a wide range of the body's organs, it may first cause joint symptoms. At some point in the course of their disease, almost all sufferers of SLE will have *arthralgias* (painful but not swollen or warm) joints and even frank arthritis (with swelling, pain, redness, and warmth). The arthritis may be a crippling one, and because the ligaments and tendons as well as the joint and its surrounding tissues become inflamed, the pull of the muscles and tendons can lead to a specific pattern of deformity in the feet and hands. In the hands of about one-third of SLE patients, the arthritis creates enough instability at the joint where the wrist joins the thumb (the carpometacarpal joint) to cause the thumb to jut out at an awkward angle. Physicians, who must think up a descriptive name for everything to make it easier to remember, have dubbed this deformity *hitchhiker's thumb,* and it is characteristic of SLE.

The arthritis seen in SLE often strikes both of a pair of joints, and in regard to the pattern of joints involved and to some degree the hand and foot deformities that develop, the arthritis in SLE mimics rheumatoid arthritis. However, there are X-ray and blood marker differences between the two, which we will examine a bit later when we discuss the tools of diagnosis.

And because you will very likely not have X-ray and blood work results to assist you in sorting out which of your family members and ancestors may have had SLE and which RA, let me give you some additional visible features to look for in the patient with SLE. As I said, the disease involves multiple body tissues: the skin, the kidneys, the lungs, the nervous system, and the heart.

Chief among them—because it is readily available for you to see—is the skin. People who suffer from SLE will usually have a rash that may flare up and subside for many years. In the classic case, a red, often scaly or eczematous rash breaks out in a pattern vaguely reminiscent of a butterfly lying across the nose and cheeks. An all-over-the-body, pale red rash that looks a bit like measles may accompany the *butterfly rash.* The rashes may worsen when the disease worsens and may be brought on by exposure to sunlight—natural or artificial, such as a tanning bed.

In identifying members among your family who may have had

SLE, look for arthritis particularly involving the hands and feet, the butterfly rash, and often chronic and sometimes quite serious problems with the lungs and the kidneys (the latter case usually involving the passage of blood or protein in the urine that is unrelated to a urine infection) that may lead to high blood pressure.

You have just learned a good bit about several of the most common arthritides and now know that what we speak of as *arthritis* encompasses a diverse group of inherited joint diseases. Because of their diversity, demographic analysis of high-risk groups is anything but straightforward. Identifying those groups likely to be targets becomes a complex issue, because whether a particular segment of society is at greater risk for an arthritic disease depends on the disease in question. Is there no simple description of *the person* at risk for arthritis, no quick checklist to tell us who will it strike and when? Let's see.

## Who's at Risk: The Demographics of Arthritis

Look at a clock. Does it have a second hand? If it does, watch as it ticks off one minute and six seconds. During that short space of time, two more Americans developed some form of arthritis. Statistics compiled by the Arthritis Foundation tell us that 1 million new cases of arthritis will occur this year in the United States alone—that's one new case every thirty-three seconds. In the amount of time it takes to watch a TV commercial or to microwave a corn dog, another person will develop an arthritic disease. Who are these million Americans? Is the target group male? Female? Black? White? Young? Old? The answer is a resounding: it depends. Let me illustrate with examples. In regard to:

*Gender (Sex).* In many of the arthritides, women significantly outnumber men, but the reverse is true in gout, ankylosing spondylitis, and Reiter's syndrome. Some of the childhood forms of arthritis occur equally often in boys and girls, yet in others, one sex predominates. In general,

Females represent:

- Three-fourths of the patients with rheumatoid arthritis.
- Twice as many cases of osteoarthritis.
- Nine times more patients with systemic lupus.
- Seven times more cases of juvenile rheumatoid arthritis.

Males, on the other hand, account for:

- About four times more cases of ankylosing spondylitis.
- More than three-fourths of patients with gouty arthritis.
- At least a five times greater incidence of Reiter's syndrome.

*Race.*

- Caucasians develop more cases of ankylosing spondylitis, as do certain Native American populations (Chippewa, Pima, Haida, and others); however, the disease is exceedingly rare in African blacks and Japanese.
- Caucasians and, again, some of the Native American populations (in particular, the Yakima and Mille-Lac Chippewa) also develop rheumatoid arthritis with greater frequency than do American blacks or native Asians (both Chinese and Japanese).
- Blacks, Asians (particularly Chinese and Filipino), and Hispanics account for more cases of systemic lupus erythematosus.
- Filipinos, Polynesians, and the Maori of New Zealand tend to have higher levels of uric acid in their blood, and consequently suffer more gouty arthritis—whether this effect is entirely racial or in large measure dietary, is debatable, and gouty arthritis occurs in all ethnic subgroups with great regularity.
- There appears to be no certain racial effect for osteoarthritis or juvenile rheumatoid arthritis.

*Age.*

- Rheumatoid arthritis typically strikes between the ages of twenty and fifty, but can develop at any age.
- Systemic lupus occurs primarily in the childbearing years (ages fifteen to fifty-five).
- Most cases of ankylosing spondylitis begin between ages sixteen and thirty-five.
- The first attacks of gout typically occur in the forty- to fifty-year age group, but can begin earlier; in women, the disease rarely begins before menopause.
- In osteoarthritis—the wear-and-tear arthritis that we associate with aging—the symptoms usually do not become manifest until age forty to forty-five in men and a bit later in women (fifty-five to sixty); however, those joints that have received greater trauma (from accident or misuse) may be stricken at even earlier ages.

*Obesity.*

- More cases of osteoarthritis occur in the excessively overweight for the obvious reason that their joints must chronically bear more weight and, therefore, receive more daily trauma.
- Again, because the chief promoter of gouty arthritis is dietary excess, obese individuals generally suffer a higher incidence of gout than the lean population.

As you can see from these examples, to try to pinpoint a single high-risk population for the arthritides would create more confusion than clarity. The questions then become: How can you assess your personal risk? How do you decide whether you or your children indeed *are* at risk for an arthritis? Will you be among the million Americans to develop some form of arthritis this year? The single best predictor of disease is family history. Does arthritis tend to run in your family? If so, you may be— just as I am—at greater risk for developing one of these diseases. If you think you may be, follow along with me as we examine the genetics of arthritis.

# 2

# The Inheritance Factor

**A Self Test for Arthritis Risk**
Answer the following questions that will begin to help you gain
a clearer picture of your own risk for developing arthritis:

1. Do you have arthritic family members? _____
2. Are they male or female? _____
3. On the side of one parent or both? _____
4. What kind of arthritis do, or did, they have? _____
   _____
5. What joints or groups of joint seemed most affected? ____
   _____
6. At what age did they develop their disease? _____
7. Did their disease come and go or was it constant? _____
8. Did they develop crippling and deformity? _____

Although you may not know the answers to all these questions
about your family's arthritis history right now, it's time to begin

your search. Question anyone who might know about arthritis among your family members: your parents, brothers and sisters, grandparents, aunts and uncles, cousins, and family friends. Trace back as far into your heritage as you are able. You will use this kind of information to construct a family genogram (much like a family pedigree) later in this chapter. The genogram will illustrate for you—in a clear and concise manner—the lines along which arthritic diseases have traveled through the successive generations of your family and will help you determine if you or your children are at risk for arthritis. If you believe you may be, as you proceed with your family medical search, you will want to understand how the genetic message for arthritis is passed on, so let's examine that aspect now.

## The Passage of Inherited Messages

Although physicians—even the very earliest healers such as Hippocrates and Galen in ancient Greece and Rome—had recognized the family clustering of cases of various types of joint disease, a true understanding of the specific mode of inheritance of arthritis susceptibility has come about relatively recently. In fact, about all that physicians understood about the inheritance of rheumatoid arthritis when my father developed it in the mid-1960s, for example, was that it *could* run in the family. No medical test to detect those family members who might be at greater risk could yet be done, and no certain understanding of what might prompt susceptible family members to develop the disease yet existed.

While medical science still does not have all the answers, researchers have compiled a veritable mountain of new information about these diseases and their heritability. As we proceed, you will be better able to understand how this susceptibility to develop a disease such as arthritis passes from one generation to the next, if I first give you a brief and very basic overview of genetics. (Some of you may already be familiar with how traits pass from parent to child, but you may want to review the basics.)

### The Basic Rules of Genetics Beginning with "Birds Fly"

My mother taught English at our local high school for years. She was frequently disliked by her students, because she was exacting and demanded the best they could give. But she was very nearly always beloved by her *former* students, because when she had finished with them, they could write, and write reasonably well. After the dust settled, they could better appreciate her for giving them the most important tool they would need for college—the ability to put their thoughts in written form—by drumming into them a real understanding of the construction of sentences. Students groaned when they realized they had been assigned to Mrs. Crane's Composition 401, because her reputation for toughness was legend. Students viewed her class as difficult and time-consuming, because she made them write, and write, and write. And she made suggestions and corrections to improve their writing all over the pages and filled the margins with red ink. Their first compositions looked as though she had slashed her wrists and bled on them. But their writing invariably improved.

She used to laugh at her "hard teacher" reputation, saying that she even began her honors senior composition students with the bare basics. She would say, "We begin with a simple sentence: Birds fly. Now how hard can this class be?" This disclaimer was true; I know this as fact, because I was one of those students in my senior year, and we indeed began the composition semester as she promised, with "Birds fly." Thereafter, she built on that basic framework of the simplest complete sentence made up of a one-word subject and one-word predicate until we all were able to construct passable—albeit, not deathless—prose.

And so I will begin now at the "Birds fly" level with you in your short course in genetics. First, I'll introduce you to the chromosomes and genes that store the genetic information and dictate to a large degree what we become, then we'll move on through the basic rules of genetics that—although on a much more complex scale—govern the inheritance of diseases such as the arthritides, and ultimately on to examine the genetic message that makes some of us better targets for their development. Although the field of medical genetics is enormously complex, if I can distill it down to the basic truths of inheritance, right down to the "Birds fly" level, even those readers who have little scientific background—and perhaps believe they have even less interest in it—will finish this section with a clearer understanding of the basic process of inheritance.

### Chromosomes, Genes, and Inheritance

Your genes control virtually everything about you, from the color of your hair, skin, and eyes to the size of your feet and to whether you have attached ear lobes or floppy ones. The controlling messages pass from parent to child in the chromosomes. So let's begin at the obvious beginning point: What is a chromosome? What is a gene?

Think of chromosomes as tiny spools of information, much like little computer tapes, that contain huge amounts of data. Geneticists studying them have arranged them by size and for convenience have numbered them one through twenty-three, going from the largest to the smallest. The chromosomes in reality are made up of precisely wound strands of a special genetic protein called deoxyribonucleic acid (DNA), which in turn is made up of millions and millions of subunits called bases or base-pairs. The bases function much like Morse code signals, because they line up in a very specific order that when "read" determines an encoded message meaningful to anyone or anything capable of understanding the code.

*Where do they come from?*   If we go all the way back to the moment of our conception, an egg cell, or ovum, carrying twenty-three of these chromosomes contributed by our mother, combines with a sperm cell, carrying the twenty-three chromosomes contributed by our father. The newly formed cell created by the union of the egg and the sperm is called a *zygote*. This single-celled zygote now contains a complete set of forty-six chromosomes, representing one pair of each of the twenty-three chromosomes. This first cell possesses all of the preprogrammed chemical (genetic) information needed to develop a whole new human being, different from all others, with every physical trait that it inherits developing as a result of the genetic messages contained on its strands of DNA. For some of us, one of the millions of messages passed along may be an increased susceptibility for developing arthritis or other diseases.

But, back to the zygote. As the single cell divides to make two, and the two divide to make four, and so on, the set of chromosomes duplicates and reduplicates with each division, so that the messages on the original forty-six chromosomes pass to each and every one of the cell copies. Although each of your body's cells still contains all this information in the forty-six chromosomes, along the way as different kinds of cells specialize to become only skin cells or only kidney cells or only joint-lining cells, the messages for performing all the other types of cell behavior fall silent. And after we become fully formed human beings, a skin cell can only be a skin cell—even though it still has the silent genetic knowledge to become a heart muscle cell.

Normally, only a few kinds of primitive cells in the bone marrow retain the ability to transform along different paths, and even these cannot fully express all of the silent genetic messages. (Occasionally, a few of the very primitive cells may survive as a "rest" or deposit in some tissues, particularly the ovary, to develop along bizarre lines later in life; this can create a variety of unusual benign tumors, but this behavior is considered aberrant.)

Under normal circumstances, cells receive direction about when to develop as they should and when to quit developing. The messages or signals that prompt the turning on and subsequent turning off of a cell's ability to use all the stored information—as well as messages that may trigger the development of a disease such as arthritis under the proper stimulus—also originate in controlling genes on the chromosomes.

A *gene,* on the other hand, is nothing more than a grouping of the DNA bases (maybe 40,000 or 50,000 of them per gene) in a specific location along the chromosome strand; each of them contains the codes of *one* particular message. The message, for example, may be to tell a certain type of pigment cell to make more of a special protein that makes the eyes brown or the hair black, or to stimulate bone and cartilage cells to greater growth for a longer period of time to make the individual tall. Or it might be a message that causes the cells of the nose cartilage to develop a certain way, giving it a shape like our mother's or father's, or makes us more susceptible to a disease such as arthritis. How have the scientists figured all this out? Let's see.

## A Short Course in Mendelian Genetics

Most of what we know of how traits pass through the generations—at least the basic facts—came to us through the diligent and careful work of a nineteenth-century Austrian monk named Gregor Mendel, who recorded the essential truths of dominant and recessive genetic transmission by studying the traits of peas he tended in the monastery garden. He developed a set of rules that allow us to predict the passage and expression of such traits (*expression* being the term geneticists use to refer to the end product of the genetic message that results in the traits we see, such as blue eyes or dark skin or tall stature or some diseases). We call these the rules of Mendelian inheritance in honor of Father Mendel.

In the course of his study, Father Mendel noticed that by cross-pollinating his pea plants in a controlled fashion, he could tell from the parent plants' traits how the seedling plants would develop—i.e., whether their seedpods would be wrinkled or smooth, their leaves solid colored or striped, their flowers purple or white. By keeping careful records of each generation, he developed mathematical rules to predict what kind of offspring the crossing of two parent plants would yield, which traits would always be expressed (*dominant traits*) and which ones would only be expressed if both parents passed the trait (*recessive traits*).

Although these Mendelian rules do not apply to all cases, they do form the basis for medical genetics and are, therefore, important to our understanding of the genetics of arthritis. Let me illustrate how the rules that govern the passage of traits work with a short example. If we are to begin at the "Birds fly" level, we must assume that a single gene pair controls the trait. In reality, however, the expression of many diseases—and most arthritides fall into this category—arises from the interplay and contribution of multiple gene pairs.

Let's choose as our hypothetical example the fur color of a mouse, and let's assume that the fur of this hypothetical breed of mice can only be white or gray. Remember, we are assuming that a single gene pair controls fur color. Let's say that the allele (one member of the "pair" that makes up the gene) for gray fur is the dominant allele—meaning that it will always be expressed if it is present, and the mouse who carries a gene with this allele will be a gray mouse. White fur, then, will be our recessive trait (the state that occurs when neither allele codes for the gray color). In this example, we will mate a white mouse and a gray mouse and predict what the fur color of the baby mice will be.

To keep it simple, we must begin with "pure" strains, meaning that the gray-furred parent mouse has both its alleles as dominant ones for gray fur (which we will designate G and G), and the white-furred parent has two recessive alleles for white fur (which we will designate g and g, using the lower case to represent the recessive form of the fur-color gene that we are calling the "G" gene). Also, for simplicity, let's assume that the pure-bred gray mouse is the male.

We now cross our parent gray mouse with its white mate:

(gray parent) $GG$—$gg$ (white parent)

The parents, you remember, will each donate only one of their two alleles for fur color to each baby mouse of their litter as follows:

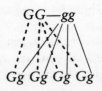

$GG$—$gg$

$Gg$ $Gg$ $Gg$ $Gg$

Because we began with pure-bred gray and white mice, the gray
father mouse could only donate dominant G genes, because that
is all he had. The same is true for the pure-bred white mother
mouse; she could only donate recessive g genes to her babies,
because that's all she had to give. The resultant litter of four
mice will *all* be gray, although each of them is a hybrid—that
is, each of the babies carries one dominant G allele from its
father and one recessive g allele from its mother. But because G
is a dominant allele, it will be expressed if it is present; therefore,
all the babies will have gray fur.

In the next generation, things can get a little more interesting,
so let's now mate two mice out of this all-gray "hybrid" litter.
These gray-furred parents will have fur color alleles like this:

$$Gg—Gg$$

Again, each parent will donate one or the other of its two alleles
to each of its offspring. If we again have four babies from this
crossing of mice, we might get any of the following combinations:

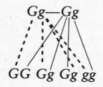

In this litter, three of the baby mice will be gray, but one will
have white fur. Why? Because of the random shuffling of the
parents' genes in the cross. Three of the mice received at least
one dominant G allele from a parent and will, therefore, have
gray fur. But one mouse happened to receive the recessive g allele
from both parents. Because it has no dominant gray G allele at
all, it will be a white mouse from two gray-furred parents.

It is precisely by this simple, direct means that such diseases
as hemophilia, sickle-cell disease, and cystic fibrosis pass from
generation to generation in humans. The vast majority of inherited arthritic diseases, however, do not obey so simple a scheme.

The susceptibility requires a more convoluted interplay of multiple genes and the promotional effect of environmental stimulators, such as trauma or infection, to finally result in expression of the genetic message—such as the development of an arthritis. And although the entire human genome is infinitely more complex, with millions of genes controlling millions of traits, the same basic truths apply. But at the "Birds fly" level, this is the mechanism by which all traits pass from one generation to the next.

Although a simple example, the appearance of a white-furred mouse from two gray parents in this scenario should also help explain from a genetic standpoint why you may sometimes see a particular trait "skip" generations, or be expressed in one child in a family, but not in others. It also points out the importance of tracing your genogram back a few generations if you can.

## Constructing Your Genogram

One of the tools I would like you to use to help you determine your risk for arthritis is the *genogram*. Think of it as a picture representation of your family tree of medical history. To begin to construct a family genogram in regard to your own risk of arthritic disease, begin with your closest relatives—your brothers and sisters, parents, aunts and uncles—and work backward to your grandparents on both sides of your family and even a generation further if you are able. If you wish to identify your child's risk of inheriting an arthritic disease, you might want to do a separate genogram that includes your husband's side of the family as well.

In preparing the "skeleton" of your family tree, you can use the standard genogram symbols recommended by the Task Force of the North American Primary Care Research Group and described in *Genograms in Family Assessment* by Monica McGoldrick and Randy Gerson. Or you can invent any symbols you like—as long as you distinguish between female and male family members and between those still alive and those who have died. The standard genogram symbols are

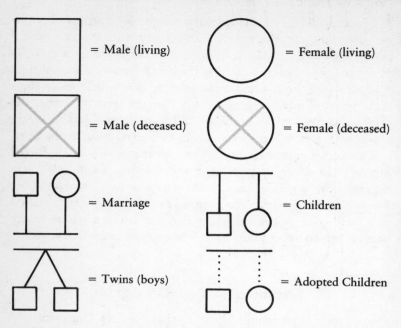

Although you may not use all of these symbols in your genogram, they will be helpful should you wish to construct other genograms to track various other aspects of your family's medical history.

In addition to these basic symbols, you may want to draw a double line around yourself to distinguish yourself from the rest of your family. Fill in everyone's name and year of birth, as well as the year of death for anyone who has died. When you have finished drawing the skeleton of your family tree, you will have a diagram that resembles Figure 2. Once you have this skeleton, you can begin adding the specific notes that will help you trace your family history of arthritis.

Be as thorough as you can in adding—to one side of each person's symbol—what you readily know about the occurrence of arthritis among your relatives, which may be quite a lot or very little. Include, if you can, the pattern of joints involved that I discussed previously (i.e., did their arthritis mainly affect hips, knees, ankles, wrists, total length of spine, spine in the neck or

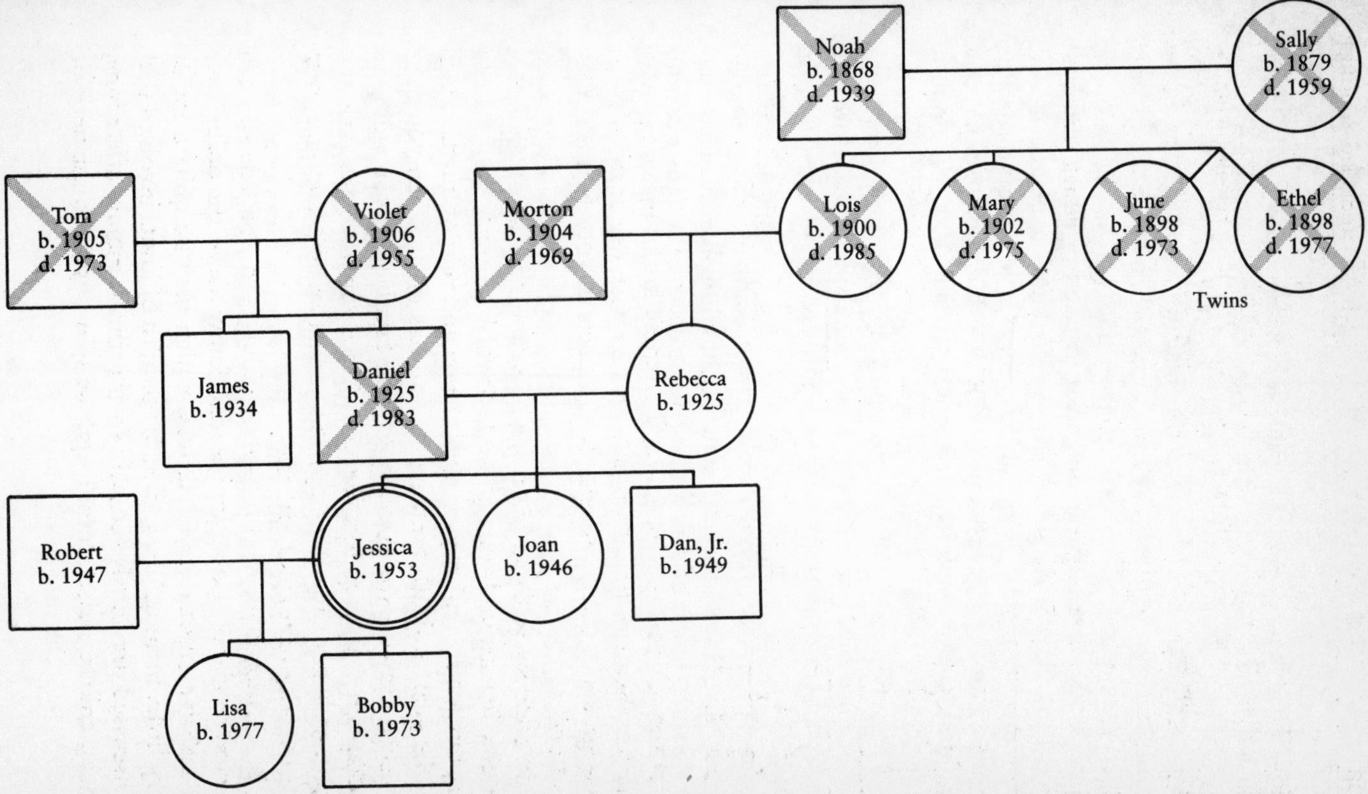

Figure 2. "Jessica's" Family Tree, Genogram #1.

lower back alone, etc.), the time in life (adolescence, adulthood, or late in life) when the arthritis developed, and whether or not the relative also suffered such related conditions as the skin rash found in psoriasis, the butterfly rash of lupus, or the bowel problems seen in ulcerative colitis and Crohn's disease. Refer to the descriptions of the various arthritides in chapter 1 to help you decide on a possible diagnosis in cases in which you have no clear medical diagnosis. If you *do* know a diagnosis with certainty, designate it by underlining it; you should also indicate your own "presumptive" or possible diagnoses in some manner, for example, with a question mark, as was done in Figure 3.

The genograms will help you pick out a pattern of arthritic occurrence that you may not have ever recognized before, but that could be important additional information in assessing your risk.

Don't be discouraged if you cannot complete the genogram right away. As you read through this and the subsequent chapters and gain a clearer understanding of the diseases and their various risk factors, you should return to the chart and fill in any new information that you have gleaned from your research.

Also, you may have noted in Figure 3 that I have listed habits, such as high-sugar diet, significant alcohol use, the presence of allergies, and whether or not the relative sustained a major joint trauma or suffered from obesity. These are examples of the environmental risk factors about which you will learn in chapter 3, devoted entirely to that subject. After you have read that chapter, you should have a better understanding of what kind of habits to look for that may have been important to the development and course of arthritis in your family members. So, don't worry yet about filling such habits in; you can come back to the genogram to add this kind of information later.

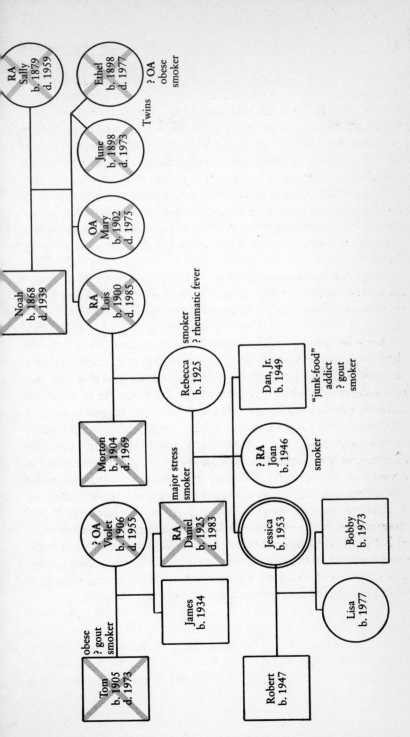

Figure 3. "Jessica's" Family Tree, Genogram #2.

## The Genetics of Arthritis

I have already said that medical researchers know that the inheritance of arthritis does not exactly follow the simple rules laid down by Father Mendel, so let's take a look at the way in which genetics specialists *do* believe those of us at risk inherit the message.

The direction we must turn for our answer is to the genes controlling our body's immune (disease-fighting) system, which lie in an area on chromosome 6. Geneticists refer to this grouping of genes by one of two names: the major histocompatibility complex (MHC) or the human leukocyte antigen system (HLA system). The genes along this area carry the coded information to help us recognize our own body's tissues as "self" and anything else that might choose to invade us—i.e., a bacterium; a virus; a transplanted liver, heart, or kidney; or transfused blood—as "nonself." The response to almost anything that falls into the nonself category is a full-frontal assault by our immune system, which seeks out the invader, mounts a killing response against it, and destroys it, if possible. This defensive mechanism, gone haywire, may in part explain how the extraordinary inflammation in arthritis occurs.

Scientists studying the MHC have learned how to "type" the various regions along the gene group, with technology that has opened up the field of organ transplantation. Through "typing" the MHC, physicians searching for a "new" heart or kidney for a dying patient know in advance whether a donor organ will "match." If the match of MHC genes is a close one, the patient's ever-vigilant immune system will be much less likely to view the new organ as nonself and destroy it. What, you may be wondering at this point, does all this have to do with arthritis? Bear with me—here's the connection.

In the case of some diseases, such as the various forms of inherited arthritis, specific portions of the MHC carry certain genetic information that, if triggered, can cause the MHC immune team mistakenly to view legitimate body tissues—such as the synovial joint lining or tendon and ligament fibers—as nonself, and the war begins. The trigger tips the first domino and sets in motion the cascade of inflammation and joint destruction that I discussed earlier. Researchers have dubbed these kinds of diseases in which the body's defense system appears to turn on itself *autoimmune diseases.*

As you will remember from the short course in genetics, each of our parents has *two copies* of chromosome 6, each of which has the genes of the MHC. And so our genetic makeup in this respect represents information contributed by both our parents. Because the MHC contains many subunits along its course, the number of possible combinations of these genes would be limitless in theory were it not for a clever twist. The regions very rarely separate into fragments, but pass as a whole, allowing for the traceable passage of the immune system gene groups from parent to child. Were it not for this fact, "matching" of immune markers on transplanted organs could not occur, because the possible combinations of the immune area that *could* result when the genetic cards are shuffled would make even a parent and child immunologically dissimilar. And as you recall, an immune system would instantly recognize a "nonmatched" transplanted organ as nonself and destroy it. Fortunately, such is not the case, because the regions and subregions of the MHC area pass largely intact from parent to child.

The MHC genes "code" for the production of specific immune system molecules that coat the surfaces of all the cells in the body, acting as markers, or flags, that tell other immune system cells that this cell is one of "us," i.e., self and not nonself. Immunogeneticists (scientists specializing in the study of the inheritance of immune functions) group these immune molecules into two distinct classes: Class I and Class II. They further subdivide these two classes into a total of six main subclasses: Class I into HLA-A, HLA-B, and HLA-C and Class II into HLA-DP, HLA-DQ, and HLA-DR subregions. (The names in these subclasses use the HLA—human leukocyte antigen—designation, so don't let that confuse you. Remember the HLA system is synonymous with the MHC.) The Class I markers cover the surfaces of virtually all the types of cells in our bodies—muscle cells, skin cells, liver cells, heart-lining cells, and on and on. The Class II markers, however, primarily only coat certain types of white blood cells, which are involved in the recognition of invaders.

Over the millennia, subtle shifts created by occasional errors in recopying the genetic message from cell to cell and by exposure to various infecting invaders—such as viruses, bacteria, and fungi—have molded, colored, and altered the basic framework of the MHC. These mutations, or changes, have created hundreds of alternative gene forms that code for slightly different gene products (the immune markers we spoke about earlier). And so immunogeneticists refer to the HLA-DR4 region or the HLA-B27 region. The numbers simply indicate a slightly different gene form—HLA-DR4 still refers to the DR subregion of Class II, but also to a special type of DR immune molecule that has been designated "4." There are also DR immune molecules with the numbers 1, 2, 3, 5, 6, 7, etc. It is these markers—different ones for different diseases—that we correlate with genetic susceptibility for the arthritides. Notice, once again, that I say *susceptibility* for, because the markers also occur in some people who do not have, and possibly never will have, an arthritic disease. These markers just occur with much higher frequency in people who do have an arthritic disease.

For example, rheumatoid arthritis patients will often have immune markers from the DR subregion on their cells, especially the DR4 region. Patients with SLE (lupus disease) will often exhibit the DR2 marker; and AS patients, the B27 marker. Although physicians rarely need to check for these markers in the blood of patients suffering from an arthritic disease—clinical findings, joint patterns, and other less-exotic blood tests will usually identify the cause—the testing can be done on family members of known sufferers to help assess risk. Again, I caution you to bear in mind that having the marker does not confer the disease; it does, however, confer a susceptibility for developing the disease. I would urge any patient who has such a marker—or a family history that strongly suggests an inherited arthritis—to take stock of their physical condition today and to make the necessary changes in lifestyle to ensure soundness of body, mind, and immune system. Certainly, putting your body and immune system into the best possible shape can do no harm, and it may be your best defense against falling victim to the messages in your genes.

## Genetic Research and the Future

Advances in genetic research technology in recent years have made it possible for scientists to identify specific genes that may be involved in causing certain cancers, some nervous system diseases, and recently even genes that may promote heart disease, cholesterol problems, and obesity. This same kind of research has also yielded the important discoveries about the MHC and the genes that make us susceptible to arthritis. But, immunogeneticists have only scratched the tip of the iceberg in genetic research. The vast and largely unexplored frontier of the human gene pool awaits discovery.

Congress has recently entered the arena of genetics, by last year earmarking $62 million to finance the Human Genome Project; our lawmakers have also pledged another $3 billion to continue this work over the next fifteen years. The aims of this collaboration of gene researchers are to identify and locate each of the 50,000 to 100,000 individual human genes that comprise the human genome and to decipher the information they contain. Perhaps with luck and diligence, this project may lead to the unlocking of the secrets of inherited diseases.

Once medical scientists understand how the genome works, they may be able to *predict* with certainty who is at risk for an illness, such as arthritis. The practical application of these discoveries, at that point, will lie in identifying high-risk patients. For example, the genetics specialists could test family members of arthritis victims by examining their chromosomes to see if they, too, have the immune system genes that would indicate a higher risk for arthritis. To some degree, these tests can already be done, although they rarely are. As I have already said, blood tests can readily identify those patients with the genetic markers that may indicate susceptibility for a number of arthritic diseases,* in particular AS, RA, Reiter's syndrome, and SLE. Those young people at higher risk could then begin to make informed lifestyle decisions early on about what they eat, whether they drink alcohol, how closely they maintain their ideal weight, etc., all of which I will examine with you in subsequent chapters.

Genetic risk knowledge only has value, after all, if there is something that can be *done* about the disease—i.e., some way to prevent its occurrence or a better chance for cure if it is discovered earlier. Simply telling patients that they carry the genes to develop a debilitating disease for which there is no hope for prevention or cure certainly benefits no one. However, for arthritic diseases, in which lifestyle changes may reduce risk for development and in which early diagnosis and prompt treatment *can and do* affect the outcome by preventing crippling, genetic screening tests would be a help. These kinds of new discoveries in genetics and chromosome research may have far-reaching effects for the future diagnosis and treatment not only of the arthritides but of many other inherited diseases as well.

## Interpreting Your Genogram: What Does It Mean?

I want to insert a note of caution right at the beginning of this section. The chief purpose of constructing your genogram is to illustrate more clearly your inherited risk of developing arthritis, not to alarm you in any way. Discovering that this, or any disease for that matter, occurs with greater frequency in your family could be upsetting. And so I want you to keep in mind—I realize I've said it a hundred times so far—that *inheriting a risk does*

---

*Medical laboratories can already identify the antigens of the MHC by blood and tissue tests. Arthritic specialists around the country can, and often do, test family members to identify the presence of the antigens that confer susceptibility to arthritic diseases. If you would like to know more about this testing consult your family physician or contact the Arthritis Foundation.

*not mean inheriting the disease.* Knowing your risk *does,* however, give you the opportunity to *do something* about it. So forge ahead with me, and let's make a realistic appraisal of your situation, so that whatever your risk may be, in subsequent chapters you can learn the positive steps you can take to improve it.

Once you have completed your family genogram, step back and take a look at its patterns and again answer the questions at the start of the chapter. If you recognize a pattern of one or more of the arthritides recurring in generation after generation, you may be at higher risk. If you can track the *same type* of arthritis as it is passed along in a direct chain—for example, from your great-grandparent to your grandparent to your parent—you can assume that that tendency may indeed have been passed on to your generation as well. The possibility places you and your brothers and sisters at higher risk to develop that kind of arthritis.

Depending on the arthritic disease in question—if you will recall your minitutorial on genetics—the possibility also exists that the set of MHC genes that you received from your parents— even from a parent with arthritis—might *not* be the ones associated with the development of the disease. The random shuffling of the genetic cards may have dealt you an arthritis-free hand. In many inherited arthritides, MHC typing can verify the presence or absence of the gene markers that would indicate a susceptible immune makeup; however, these tests are not yet routinely performed merely to screen family members, largely because they are expensive. However, these kinds of tests *are* available, and you may wish to confer with your family physician about whether you could benefit from such a test. For those of you who have such an interest, I have included a list of the MHC markers usually associated with the different arthritic conditions in Table 1 (page 48).

Although I would like to be able to give you a specific percentage or a number to quantify your risk of inheriting an arthritic disease—for example, to say one-fourth of those with one parent or one-half of those with two parents will develop thus-

Table 1. MHC Markers Commonly Associated with Some Arthritides*

| Disease | Primary Marker | Other Markers | Relative Risk |
|---|---|---|---|
| Ankylosing spondylitis | B27 | | 69.1 |
| Bowel disease spondylopathies | B27 | | 10.2 |
| Psoriatic arthritis | B27 | B38, Bw16, B17 | 7.8 |
| Reiter's syndrome | B27 | | 37.1 |
| Rheumatoid arthritis | DR4 | DR1 | 2.7 |
| Systemic lupus erythematosus | DR2 | | 2.3 |

*Note: Neither gouty arthritis nor osteoarthritis seem to have a specific correlated MHC marker. Adapted from the *Primer on Rheumatic Diseases,* R. Schumacher, J. Klippel, and D. Robinson, eds., 9th edition, Atlanta: Arthritis Foundation, 1988, p. 199.

and-so disease—such clear-cut patterns do not occur in the arthritides. What I can give you, however, is information about the *relative risk* that people who inherit the various genetic MHC markers for a specific disease carry. You must again remember that inheriting a disease tendency and developing a disease are two different things.

First, let me explain what I mean by a *relative risk.* Research scientists determine this value by taking the people with a particular disease and dividing those who carry a marker for it by the number of those who don't have that marker. They then compare this ratio to people—with and without the marker—that *don't* have the disease. This calculation gives some indication of how reliable a marker, such as MHC typing, is in predicting risk for a disease. The higher the relative risk number, the greater its association with the disease. A relative risk of *one* means *no* association whatsoever. I have added the relative risk of the various arthritides to Table 1.

High-risk families will clearly benefit from maintaining fitness through careful attention to nutrition, proper exercise and physical conditioning, and routine health maintenance, which I will address in the following chapters.

If you do *not* find any of these patterns, your genetic risk for arthritis is probably not increased above normal. Although your family gene pool does not place you at higher risk for the inherited arthritides, you may still want to examine the information on lifestyle and nutrition for other health reasons, because you can derive nothing but good from building a sound, healthy body and immune system.

# 3

# Environmental Triggers of Arthritis

In the first two chapters of this book, I have remarked time and again that although we who are at risk do inherit a genetic *susceptibility* for developing arthritis, an additional triggering stimulus must occur for that potential to become a reality. Research has pointed the finger at various culprits in this regard, but the majority of these triggers hail from the germ world— i.e., bacteria, viruses, or the like. Medical scientists over the years have correlated the appearance of certain of the arthritides with a higher degree of frequency than one should expect, following infections by some organisms. But infectious triggers alone cannot account for all cases of arthritic disease, and consequently, those who study these diseases have continued to probe for other common denominators—such as trauma, chemicals, food allergies, malnutrition, and specific nutritional deficiencies—as possible stimulators. Some of the theories enjoy general acceptance among medical scientists, whereas others are still swathed in tangles of medical controversy.

Together, you and I will explore the most widely studied theories and, I hope, make some sense of the chaos, most especially that involving the claims about the beneficial and/or deleterious effects of nutrition, which we will cover in the next chapter. Turn with me now and examine the various triggers—and reputed triggers—of arthritic diseases that scientists have so far uncovered.

## Germ Warfare: Infectious Triggers of Arthritis

Let's begin here, with the microbes that scientists postulate may be triggers of the genetic message for arthritic diseases. Again, because we must deal with a constellation of diseases lumped together under the label *arthritis,* we must remember that whether or not an infectious agent acts as a trigger depends largely on which arthritic disease you look at. And although the causative organisms vary, the scenario remains much the same.

In most instances, the triggering impetus probably arises from confusion on the part of our immune systems in differentiating "self" from "nonself." Scientific research has demonstrated this aberrant recognition phenomenon more clearly for some diseases than for others, and as it is especially apparent in Reiter's syndrome, I propose to make that disease our starting point, and then proceed disease by disease as we did before.

### Reiter's Syndrome

Of the many theories to explain what stimulates the development of arthritic disease in those of us who are susceptible, medical studies offer no more convincing evidence than the case for infectious triggers and Reiter's syndrome—the disease complex of arthritis, urethritis, and conjunctivitis, affecting the joints, urinary tract, and eyes, respectively. You will recall from chapter 1 that this kind of arthritis was once thought solely to be a consequence of venereal infections in men. But lest I upset any readers who may have relatives, spouses, or friends with

Reiter's syndrome, let me hasten to make clear that the infectious trigger need not be of so potentially scandalous an origin as sexual indiscretion, but can arise from entirely innocent infections of the urinary tract, reproductive tract, or intestinal tract.

The genetic message that makes a person susceptible to developing Reiter's syndrome involves the presence of the HLA-B27 marker; you will recognize it from Table 1 in chapter 2 as a marker also present in the other spondylopathies—ankylosing spondylitis (AS), those related to the intestinal tract (ulcerative colitis and Crohn's disease), and often in psoriatic arthritis as well. Between 80 and 90 percent of patients who develop Reiter's syndrome carry this immunogenetic marker. But why and how does having the marker create susceptibility?

Medical scientists postulate that infection with certain bacterial agents triggers the immune system domino cascade I spoke of earlier. Once activated, the immune system, as is its mission, mounts an attack against the bacterial invader. The problem ensues because of similarities between some substance in the wall or coating of the bacterium (called an antigen) and the HLA-B27 marker antigens. In the confusion created by the bacterium's perceived likeness to "self," innocent body tissues come under fire. In short, the immune defense system attacks its "self."

Another entirely plausible theory that links infection with the subsequent development of arthritic disease suggests that the marker (in this case HLA-B27) may act as a "receptor site" for the bacterium. Such a receptor site would function as a "lock" and the infectious agent as a "key." The two components, acting together, would then trigger the immune system cascade.

Research has implicated a number of bacterial agents that may act as triggers; these are listed below.

*Chlamydia trachomatis.* *Chlamydia* is a very common cause of infections of the cervix and bladder in women and, most particularly, of the urethra (the tube that leads from the urinary bladder to the outside) in men and women. In one study that examined people infected by this triggering bacterium about 3 percent went on to develop the arthritic symptoms of Reiter's syndrome. Because *Chlamydia* causes more cases of sexually transmitted (venereal) urethritis than any other bacterial agent except *Neisseria gonorrhea* in the United States, the number of cases of Reiter's syndrome brought on by it will likely continue to climb.

Fortunately, treatment with some antibiotics (most particularly those of the "mycin" or tetracycline family) kills the germ, but unless diagnosed promptly, treatment may not commence quickly enough to prevent the tipping of the first of the immune chain dominoes in those susceptible to developing the arthritic syndrome. And infection with this germ can cause even more serious problems if not treated.

In the Third World countries, where there is little access to antibiotic treatments, infection with this bacterium routinely causes blindness from the cloudy scars it ultimately creates on the cornea of the eye. Although eye infections with *Chlamydia* do occur regularly in the United States, physicians here treat them promptly with antibiotic medications and prevent these serious eye complications. Before I alarm any of you who immediately recognize that I have just said conjunctivitis—a part of Reiter's syndrome—is a term for infection of the eye, let me clarify the point: infection with *Chlamydia* is not the direct cause of the conjunctivitis and other eye problems that make up one facet of the complete Reiter's syndrome complex. The eye symptoms associated with Reiter's syndrome are *inflammatory* in origin rather than *infectious,* and just like the arthritic joint symptoms, they probably result from the same case of mistaken immune identity.

*Identifying the Symptoms of Chlamydia Infection.*   Now that you've met the first culprit, what do you look for to find it? In men, infection of the urethra by *Chlamydia* usually causes noticeable symptoms of burning pain with urination and the discharge of a usually clear (but not uncommonly cloudy or colored) material from the urinary opening very soon after the infection begins, prompting them to seek medical treatment right away. But the case may not always be so obvious. Especially in women, the infection may be "silent" and not cause symptoms disturbing enough to warrant a visit to the doctor. In these cases, the infection may occur in the cervix or bladder and go on for some time without ever being treated.

The question then arises, what can you do to prevent the infection? If you know you carry the HLA-B27 marker and/or that you have a strong family risk for Reiter's syndrome, what preventive course can you follow to lessen the risk of an infection that might trigger the disease? The most obvious answer is don't become infected with *Chlamydia*. But how? Especially when I've said many people may carry silent infections?

Because the majority of cases of *Chlamydia* infections involve the genitourinary system (encompassing both the reproductive and urinary tracts), prevention of infection quite naturally revolves around safe and sensible sexual practices. If you maintain a strictly monogamous sexual relationship, and neither you nor your partner has a *Chlamydia* infection, you needn't fear contracting the disease. Many people, however, may not be monogamous, or at least may not have been so until recently. And having multiple sexual partners naturally raises the risk of encountering someone suffering a silent infection (with *Chlamydia* or a host of other sexually transmissible diseases), which they could pass to you. The use of condoms certainly will lower the likelihood of the infection's passing in this manner, just as it does for the other venereal diseases, as well as AIDS. Abstinence will do the trick, too, but that in many cases is not a viable alternative. If you have concerns about the possibility of silent infection, see your family doctor, gynecologist, or urologist.

Prompt medical evaluation of symptoms suggesting a genitourinary infection may also help lessen the chances that the immune cascade reaction will begin. I have already described the typical symptoms in men—i.e., burning with urination and a discharge of clear, cloudy, or even colored fluid from the urethra—but what about women? What symptoms should a woman watch for? Certainly an abnormal vaginal discharge should prompt a visit to the doctor, but the symptoms may be much less specific, such as a vague discomfort in the lower abdomen, mild urinary discomfort, spotting of a little bloody discharge at odd times in the menstrual cycle, or an internal discomfort during sexual intercourse. Any of these symptoms should signal a need to see your family doctor or gynecologist. Tell your physician you have concerns about *Chlamydia* and, especially if you have an arthritic family history for Reiter's syndrome, that you want to be certain you don't have a silent infection.

Most physicians who deal with general medical care or who specialize in the genitourinary tract can and will be happy to collect the specimens necessary to screen for *Chlamydia* infection. The sampling technique amounts to no more than a swabbing of the canal of the cervix or the urethra and usually takes only a few minutes to collect. The time lag for results may be from a few minutes in clinics that do the test on the premises to a week for screens sent to outside laboratories. We do these screens regularly at my clinic, and I suspect your physician can as well. Because of the pervasiveness of the disease, some physicians may even include such screening as a routine part of their yearly Pap smear and pelvic exam.

---

### Best Preventive Strategies

1. Safe and sensible sexual practices.
2. Preventive screening for "silent" infection.
3. Periodic screening during annual medical examinations for those at high risk (such as known HLA-B27 carriers).
4. Prompt medical attention to any symptoms suggestive of infection of the reproductive or urinary tract.

---

*Shigella, Salmonella, Campylobacter, and Yersinia.* Infection by these bacterial agents usually targets the intestinal tract. Most readers will be familiar with one particular member of this group, *Salmonella typhi,* which is the bacterium that causes the infamous typhoid fever—something we physicians in urban areas rarely see anymore. But any of these bacterial groups can cause severe gastrointestinal distress in the form of abdominal cramping and a watery, often even bloody, diarrhea; the infection usually occurs from eating contaminated food or water.

Under usual circumstances, in urban areas where people depend on purified or chemically treated "city" water, physicians may not see many cases of dysentery (infectious diarrhea) caused by these bugs, but sometimes circumstances are *not* usual. For instance, recent record rainfall in Texas, Oklahoma, Louisiana, and Arkansas has swollen rivers beyond their capacity. Here in Little Rock, situated on the banks of the Arkansas River, we have listened each night to the news reports on the severe flooding all along the course of the river. Even now, I can look out my window and see the Arkansas River spilled widely over its normal banks. Flood waters have destroyed hundreds of homes, and still stand waist deep or higher in thousands more. So what does this have to do with arthritis? More than you might think.

These very kinds of bacteria—particularly *Salmonella* and *Shigella*—will come right into the homes with the flood waters. As flooding disrupts septic tanks and sewage lines, the flood water becomes tainted with raw sewage. Those residents with homes relying on well water are at even higher risk for contamination of their water supply. Because of this contamination, when the flood victims reclaim their houses, they will have to sterilize meticulously the floors, walls, cabinets, furnishings, and virtually anything else that the flood engulfed. They will have to throw out most of their food not sealed in vacuum cans, because it could be contaminated. Eating contaminated food or using contaminated utensils could cause serious infectious diarrheas. And, consequently, because of the recent flooding and the certainty that some people will fail, for whatever reason, to decontaminate their belongings carefully, those of us in the medical community in these areas may soon find ourselves awash in another flood: patients suffering from dysentery. And following those intestinal infections, we are apt to see many new cases of Reiter's syndrome as well.

But what about normal circumstances? If you keep a clean

kitchen and don't live on a flood plain, how could you come into contact with any of these bugs? You might not, if you never dine out, travel, camp, or picnic. Most Americans, however, dine out regularly, and some of us—traveling salespeople, truck drivers, and anyone whose work keeps them on the road and away from home—dine out more than at home. And what of vacation or business travel? Although in reputable restaurants anywhere you should hope not to encounter contaminated food, sometimes you do. *Salmonella* species often contaminate such dishes as potato salad, slaw, or other foods with mayonnaise-based dressings left inadequately chilled for too long a time. And, although we didn't see much of it here in Arkansas, you may recall a recent scare in many parts of the country centered around outbreaks of *Salmonella* from contaminated or improperly handled eggs.

The joint and eye symptoms typical of Reiter's syndrome also may follow intestinal infection with bacteria of the *Yersinia* species. The most famous member of this bacterial species—*Yersinia pestis*—many of you may recognize as the causative agent of bubonic plague, which was spread across Europe by infected fleas. Whether that particular bug might trigger an arthritic syndrome could hardly matter, because the illness caused by it—i.e., the plague—almost always proves fatal. Its much less deadly relatives, on the other hand, are the agents that I want to discuss at this point.

Infection caused by these other *Yersinia* types usually arises—as with the other intestinal infections—from consumption of contaminated food or water. However, the disease can spread from person to person or even animal to person. The typical early symptoms that should alert you to an intestinal infection with *Yersinia* don't differ significantly from any infectious diarrhea: cramping abdominal pain and fever. However, the cramping can be severe enough to be mistaken for appendicitis. And this particular infection may also cause a mild sore throat, inflammation of the heart muscle causing aching chest discomfort, and sometimes kidney inflammation with passage of blood and protein in the urine. Some victims of *Yersinia* infection also may develop a peculiar skin disorder, called erythema nodosum, in which painful, red lumps arise on the shins. Infections of this type occur quite often in the Scandinavian countries; however, in the United States, although *Yersinia* infections certainly do occur, they are not as common as some of the other bacterial infections.

As a physician in a mainly urban setting, I see cases of *Campylobacter* food poisoning cropping up from time to time. The usual source comes from undercooked chicken dishes, or those not kept sufficiently hot—food such as fried chicken, chicken sandwiches, and chicken strips and nuggets. (Again, the symptoms of food poisoning—nausea, vomiting, diarrhea, and cramping abdominal pain—occur with *Campylobacter* infection.) Recent medical studies have implicated infection with a bacterium of the *Campylobacter* group not only as a possible trigger for arthritic conditions but also as a cause for stomach ulcers. Physicians have begun to achieve some good results on the more hard-to-heal cases of peptic or stomach ulcers by treating patients with courses of certain antibiotic medications to wipe out the silent *Campylobacter* infection.

Let me mention at this point that infection with this group of bacteria is also associated with the inflammatory bowel diseases, ulcerative colitis and Crohn's disease, and it most likely plays a role in the arthritic disease that sometimes accompanies them. About 20 percent of the patients who suffer from these chronic intestinal diseases will go on to develop arthritis of the peripheral joints, especially the knees and ankles. Another 20 percent will develop arthritis in the pelvic joints and the lower back, and of these, 20 percent will develop typical deformities of ankylosing spondylitis. It is interesting that only about half of these patients carry the HLA-B27 antigen, which is so strongly associated with the other spondylopathies.

As with Reiter's syndrome, stimulation of some kind of "silent" genetic message by the bacterial antigens in the inflamed intestine most likely triggers the development of arthritis in these patients.

And so, you see, there are a number of ways that any of us

## Best Preventive Strategies

1. Do not eat food that has not been kept at its proper temperature. Meticulously keep hot foods hot and cold foods cold until serving time.

2. Handle fresh eggs or raw chicken with care. Because of the risk of *Salmonella* contamination, wash eggs in their shells thoroughly at the time you intend to use them. Wash your hands and any bowls/utensils that you have used in preparing the raw eggs or chicken, including countertops and cutting boards, well with hot soapy water. Cook egg or chicken dishes or sauces thoroughly.

3. When you travel outside the United States—or even to rural settings within the United States—see your physician for antibiotics to prevent traveler's diarrhea. This medication will help to protect you from infection by such organisms while abroad.

4. When traveling in rural or foreign locales, take care to drink only *sealed* bottled drinks or water. Never drink water from an unknown source unless you have purification equipment or tablets along. Remember that ice is only frozen water and in many areas may be impure; the freezing process often will not kill bacteria.

5. When traveling in areas at higher risk for traveler's diarrhea (in particular Latin America, Mexico, Italy, Spain, Scandinavia) take care about eating fresh raw fruits and vegetables.

6. Do not eat any food that either looks, smells, or tastes "bad" to you. Better to err on the side of caution than to risk illness.

7. Do not ignore symptoms. At the first sign of intestinal illness, be it cramping, vomiting, or diarrhea, seek medical attention.

at risk for arthritic diseases may come into accidental contact with another group of organisms that could trigger the immune system cascade. That being the case, what can we do to prevent such an occurrence? Except in extreme circumstances—such as a natural disaster similar to the recent flooding in Arkansas—you must only exercise your common sense about most foods.

### Ankylosing Spondylitis

Although the case for an infectious trigger in AS is not as strong as for Reiter's syndrome, recent studies suggest that a link to the germ world may exist for this arthritic disease as well. Some research indicates that antigens identified from the bacterial species *Klebsiella* and *Mycoplasma* both appear to have similarities to (once again) the HLA-B27 antigen. As before, scientists theorize that these similarities may trigger the genetic message by leading the immune system to another case of mistaken identity of "self" and its consequent assault on innocent body tissues that I described for Reiter's syndrome. Or, conversely, the B27 antigen might serve as the receptor to some bacterial antigen in the "lock-and-key" mode and thus trigger the aberrant immune system response.

*Mycoplasma.* The two microbes mentioned here tend most often to cause respiratory tract illnesses, but can infect other body systems (such as the intestinal tract or even urinary tract), too. Of the two, *Mycoplasma* is by far the more common. Especially in the spring and summer months here in Arkansas, I will treat flurries of patients of all ages suffering with the lung infection—so-called atypical, or walking, pneumonia—that *Mycoplasma* causes.

Until recently, making the diagnosis of infection by this bacterium relied more on excluding other causes of lung infection than on pinpointing *Mycoplasma*. But recently, American technology has stepped to the fore and has given physicians a new screening tool to diagnose *Mycoplasma* infection rapidly and in the office. I know that many of the hospitals and clinics in Little Rock have already begun to use such tests routinely, and it may not be long before most general and family practitioners across the country will be able to test for this bacterium in their offices (even in rural settings) and have the answer in only a few minutes.

A lung infection—signaled by cough (especially one productive of phlegm) with fever and chest inflammation—should always prompt a visit to your doctor. However, those readers who know they are at high risk for developing AS should be certain to tell their doctors of their particular concern about becoming infected with *Mycoplasma* (or *Klebsiella*) and why. Then the doctor can screen for this infection if the clinical picture fits it. As before, your chances of stimulating the genetic message may increase if you let respiratory symptoms linger before seeing your physician. Prompt action, diagnosis, and treatment might make a difference for those of you at high risk for AS.

The *Mycoplasma* bug itself is a little different from many bacteria in that it has no bacterial cell wall—a strong structure that most one-celled organisms rely on to protect themselves from the outside world. *Mycoplasma* has learned to survive without this protection and, as a result, can withstand the killing effect of many very powerful antibiotics that work by preventing the bacterium from making and repairing its all-important cell wall. To destroy such a walless bacterium, physicians must turn to medications that kill the organism from within, such as the erythromycin and sulfa antibiotics.*

*Klebsiella. Klebsiella,* on the other hand, does have a cell wall, and can be identified by culture (actually growing the offending bacterium on an agar plate in the laboratory) from samples of phlegm or other infected body fluids. The simple beauty of culturing the offending bacterium from a physician's perspective lies in what follows: a process called antibiotic sensitivity testing. This means that once the laboratory has grown the culprit, it will then test the bacterium to find out precisely what antibiotic ought to kill it.

---

*Let me clarify a point that I fear may cause some confusion. Treatment with antibiotics cures the bacterial infection, but does *not* cure arthritis once established. I do not want any of you to feel that AS or any inflammatory arthritic disease could be cured by taking an antibiotic. However, keeping you at the peak of health may make you less vulnerable to develop the arthritis to which you are susceptible.

*Maintaining Your Advantage.*  Again, because the thrust of this book is prevention of arthritis, what can we at risk do to better our odds against invasion by these stimulators? Those people at higher risk for developing AS—those who have direct blood relatives with the disease or who know they carry the HLA-B27 marker antigen—should take special care to maintain healthy lungs that will be less likely to succumb to such respiratory infections.

The single most important element immediately obvious in maintaining lung health is if you smoke, stop. Simple, right? Simple in theory, yes, but in practice, much more difficult. I would like at this point to ask a moment's indulgence of my nonsmoking readers so I can speak to the smokers. If you smoke, let me ask you to join me in a simple exercise.

Take out a blank sheet of paper and a pencil. Now draw a line down the center of the paper from the top to the bottom. On the left side of the line, write down all the bad effects of smoking cigarettes. All of them, from health concerns such as heart disease; emphysema; chronic bronchitis; peptic ulcers; and cancers of the lung, voice box, esophagus, breast, stomach, mouth, etc. to the cost and inconvenience of cigarettes to the smell and the ruined clothing. Everything. Don't leave a single negative of smoking out of your list. Take your time and be thorough. Now, on the right side of the page, write down every positive or good thing that smoking does for you. I want to ask you to be very honest with yourself in doing this.

Now compare sides. How many entries could you make on the right side of the page? A single one? Perhaps, but probably not. If you were to jot down a similar list, loaded so lopsidedly with negatives about, for example, a job you were considering, you would never dream of taking it. About a house you were contemplating buying, you'd think yourself a fool to go on with such a bad proposition. About a man or woman you were seeing, you would likely divest yourself of them before the end of the day. And yet, you might choose to continue in a bad bargain, damaging and destroying your lungs with cigarettes—which most surely will happen to some degree—because you're hooked.

Study after medical study has proven that cigarette smokers certainly suffer significantly more respiratory infections than nonsmokers, and so do the children living in their households. It naturally follows that an impaired set of lungs will more easily invite infection with bacteria that could trigger arthritic disease in susceptible people. And, therefore, if you (and your children) are at higher risk for AS—or for any of the arthritides for that matter—one of the kindest and most positive steps you could make is to kick your cigarette habit as soon as possible.

Certainly, any meaningful desire to be free of tobacco addiction must come from within you. I have counseled enough patients, friends, and family members about the medical down side of smoking to know that nothing I or anyone else can say will persuade you to stop smoking until you commit yourself to the task. All I ask of those of you who are at risk for arthritis and still smoke is to think about what you're doing and why. Make your objective list of the pros and the cons. And if you decide to quit and don't know how, I've listed several places to find help in the resource chapter of this book.

---

### Best Preventive Strategies

1. Build and maintain good general health through regular exercise (see chapter 5) and proper nutrition (see chapter 4).
2. Maintain healthy lungs by stopping smoking.
3. See your doctor promptly if you develop a respiratory infection.

---

### Psoriatic Arthritis

As was the case in AS, the evidence pointing to triggering stimuli from the germ world in psoriatic arthritis is much sketchier than for Reiter's syndrome. However, the data do at least suggest that such a bacterial trigger may play a role. As you recall, one of the main features in psoriatic arthritis is the psoriasis itself: an eczema of the skin that may range from mild with nothing more than dry, rough, flaky elbows or knees to quite severe with large areas of skin and scalp covered by thick, silvery plaques of inflamed, scaly crust.

Especially in the more severe cases of psoriasis, where the scaly plaques may break open and "weep" clear tissue fluid, the normal skin barriers to infection break down. Bacteria invade and infect the damaged areas. Researchers looking for a bacterial trigger have studied the possibility that chronic, low-level infection of the psoriatic scales—most often with Group A streptococcal-type bacteria—might be the triggering impetus to the development of the arthritis that sometimes occurs in these patients.

The genetic messages that create the susceptibility to develop arthritis in this disease do not appear to arise from a consistent area on the MHC. Immunogeneticists have correlated antigens of a number of HLA types—A1, B16, B17, B39, Cw6, DR7, DR4, and our old friend B27—with the occurrence of psoriatic arthritis.

If indeed the bacterial antigens do stimulate the awakening of the dormant genetic message, then keeping the psoriatic skin condition under control becomes an even more important task. Maintaining healthy skin, free of scale (therefore, less likely to succumb to infection by triggering bacteria), requires diligent and vigilant care by the psoriasis sufferer and the treating physician. Although those of us in the primary care fields—general and family medicine and pediatrics—regularly treat mild to moderately severe cases of psoriasis, the specialists in this regard, of course, are the dermatologists, and it is probably they who should be called on to treat the severe cases.

The mainstays of therapy—sulfur- or pine tar-based shampoos and soaps, topical steroid (cortisone-type) creams and ointments, and occasional doses of cortisone in pill or shot form—will usually suffice to keep the scaling under control. Sunlight exposure helps to clear the psoriatic eczema and in the more severe cases, dermatologists will use regimens combining an artificial source of one component of sunlight (the ultraviolet light of the "A" type wavelength) with a medication taken orally (psoralen) that increases the skin's responsiveness to the sunlight. Physicians speak of this regimen as PUVA (POO-vuh), the *P* standing for psoralen and the *UVA* standing for ultraviolet A light. This treatment will usually clear even stubborn cases of psoriasis over time. Good skin hygiene is also important for those with psoriatic eczema.

---

### Best Preventive Strategies

1. Maintain healthy, supple skin through good hygiene and sound nutrition (see chapter 4).
2. If you suffer from psoriasis or other eczematous skin problems, follow your physician's advice carefully to keep the condition under control to help maintain your skin's natural barrier to invasion by bacterial triggers.

---

### Rheumatoid Arthritis

And so we arrive again at my father's nemesis, RA. Are there also some invaders from the germ world that act to trigger the genetic message that sets this disease into motion? Again, the answer is yes, but like AS, the issue is far from settled. Researchers have proposed a number of infectious triggers from the bacterial and, more particularly, from the viral ranks, which makes the issue of prevention a more difficult prospect.

The most famous, or I should say infamous, potential triggering agent for RA is the Epstein-Barr virus, which you may recognize as the one responsible for infectious mononucleosis (the "kissing" disease so common to teenagers). Infection by this virus—which spreads person to person by saliva contact usually shared through eating, drinking, kissing, and close conversation—can cause a wide spectrum of symptoms, among them: profound fatigue, high fever, severe tonsillitis, a generalized rash over the body, headaches, muscle and joint aches, liver inflammation, enlarged spleen, abdominal pain, cough, anemia, and on and on. And the symptoms may wax and wane over periods of four to six weeks to even four to six months or more.

Although over the years researchers have looked at a number of treatment regimens for mononucleosis, no medication has yet proven of any certain value in stopping this virus. But we must remember that, with a very few exceptions—the herpes simplex virus, the varicella virus (which causes chicken pox), the influenza type A virus, and to some degree the AIDS virus—medical science has yet to develop any medication that safely and effectively eradicates viral invaders. The host immune system alone bears the burden of containing and destroying most viruses; the net effect is that the patient heals himself.

But what, if anything, can you do to prevent such an illness? How can you avoid this potential trigger if you haven't already suffered from it? Certainly first among the preventive measures would be scrupulous avoidance of sharing saliva with anyone you do not know well enough to be certain they do not currently carry the Epstein-Barr virus. Because the primary target age group for mononucleosis is five to fifteen, those of us at higher risk for RA should be cautious about direct salivary contact with our children, nieces, nephews, and our friends who are ill. However, because the virus can wax and wane and because it can persist for many months—sometimes transmissible for as long as a year after the initial illness—you cannot be ensured that someone who has had it is free from it just because they seem well at present.

Some of you may now be thinking: Aha! Now here's this doctor urging all of us who may be at risk for arthritis to take great care in trying to avoid such infectious contact, when her profession puts her into direct contact with patients known to be infected with mononucleosis. Shouldn't she practice what she's preaching? And, of course, you're right. But because my family history puts me at higher risk, just as may be the case for you, I have always tried to take extreme care in avoiding contact with the saliva, blood, or other body fluids of my patients. I do so not only because of the risk of coming into contact with the Epstein-Barr virus or some other potential promoter for arthritis but also because of occupational exposure to other, deadlier viruses such as hepatitis B or the human immunodeficiency (AIDS) viruses.

And so I caution you to take care in exposing yourselves to such illnesses, but when you do, remember that all of them—AIDS included—do not pass by casual contact. You needn't become paranoid about contracting some infectious trigger to the point that you avoid normal social and professional interaction. That said, then what are those of us at risk to do?

---

### Best Preventive Strategies

1. Maintain proper nutrition.
2. Even when "too busy," stick to a regular exercise schedule.
3. Supplement your diet with essential fats and minerals (see chapter 4 on nutrition).
4. Avoid body fluid (including saliva) contact outside your family.

---

Maintain a healthy, strong, functional immune system. A good offense through a strong defense becomes the key to fending off or withstanding any viral (or bacterial or fungal) assault. You will recall that in chapter 1, I stated that poor general health and inadequate nutrition and sanitation were chief among the reasons that RA struck so many among the poor of industrialized Europe in the late eighteenth and nineteenth centuries. A weakened, beleaguered immune system will succumb to infectious attack much more easily, potentially opening the door for the development of RA in those who carry the genetic message. But because we will examine the roles of nutrition and exercise in building, promoting, and maintaining fitness of the body *and* the mind in much greater depth in the next and subsequent chapters, let's move on.

### Systemic Lupus Erythematosus

Among the many factors studied that might promote the development of SLE, the strongest evidence points to noninfectious environmental promoters such as sunlight, burns, and other trauma. And although the genetic message that creates susceptibility to this disease may be passed along the MHC with the HLA-DR2 marker, to date, no specific bacterial or viral triggers have been proposed in the development of SLE. However, researchers have uncovered some intriguing facts that may begin to point in that direction.

There is one fairly strong bit of evidence backing a possible bacterial triggering theory for SLE. Researchers have discovered that certain types of antibodies (which are immune molecules normally built to order by the body to attack and destroy invaders such as bacteria, viruses, fungi, foreign tissues, etc.) develop not only in patients with the disease but in the blood relatives *and* nonblood relatives with whom they live. These same kinds of antibodies sometimes also develop in medical laboratory personnel who work with the blood of SLE patients. Because the body develops such antibodies to defend itself against invasion by infectious agents, their discovery in unrelated individuals certainly points to there being some sort of infective organism—possibly even an as yet unrecognized one—at work.

Medical science gives us yet another, albeit less direct, bit of evidence to suggest that a viral culprit may be at work in SLE. Patients who suffer from SLE develop other immune defense system imbalances. Their white blood cell (infection fighter cell) counts and other components of the immune cascade often drop to low levels that leave the patient more vulnerable to infection. This circumstance is not unlike the immunosuppressive effect of the HIV (AIDS) virus—although to a much less significant degree. Let me underscore that I do not intend to imply that a connection between these two diseases exists. My point is simply that similar parts of the body's defense system suffer, to a mild degree in the immune dysfunction seen in SLE and, unfortunately, to a lethal degree in the immune destruction of AIDS. This common ground and the fact that medical scientists have already pinpointed the virus responsible for the immune system assault in AIDS gives rise to the possible existence of another, similar, but less deadly, virus in such diseases as SLE.

These are intriguing data, certainly, but far from conclusive evidence that such an agent stimulates the disease. Because a stronger case exists for environmental triggers, let's take a look at these.

*Thermal Injury to the Skin.* Research implicates skin injury—caused by heat sources from too much sunlight to burns from fire or chemicals—in the development of SLE. Skin dam-

---

### Best Preventive Strategies

1. Avoid prolonged exposure to strong, direct, sunlight if possible.
2. If you do enjoy outdoor recreation, always wear a protective waterproof sunblock with an SPF rating of at least thirty when enjoying such activities as swimming, sailing, water or snow skiing. Also wear a wide-brimmed hat and protective clothing when feasible, such as when hiking, biking, or "spectating" at sports events.
3. Treat even small burns properly: immerse the burned part in cold water immediately. Take care in using butter or oily "burn" ointments and sprays, which may worsen the thermal injury. Seek medical attention immediately for a burn larger than a few centimeters, and for any burn that forms blisters.

aged by light, heat, or chemicals releases biochemical messengers that incite an inflammatory response—in effect perhaps tipping the first domino in the immune cascade. In susceptible people, the cascade may go awry, overstepping its "normal" bounds and triggering the expression of a silent genetic message: the development of SLE.

*Triggering Medications.*   Some medications appear to trigger the onset of a disease complex quite similar to SLE by a mechanism not entirely clear. The fact that many thousands of patients—the overwhelming majority—who take these drugs do *not* develop a lupuslike syndrome leads us naturally back to the assumption that it only happens in those people susceptible by virtue of their genetic preprogramming. Perhaps, once again, these medications somehow tip the first domino.

The drugs physicians most commonly associate with the lupuslike syndrome are


- **Isoniazid.** A medication used to treat tuberculosis.
- **Hydralazine.** A blood pressure lowering drug.
- **Procainamide.** A drug used to treat heart rhythm problems.
- **Chlorpromazine.** A medication variously used for nausea and vomiting, migraine headache, and psychotic agitation.
- **Certain anticonvulsant** (seizure or epilepsy) **medications.**


In many cases, the lupuslike symptoms clear and disappear once the person stops taking the offending drug. However, on occasion, the symptoms of SLE remain permanently. In these cases, the drug may act as the "key" to the immune system "lock," which opens the lid to a Pandora's box of arthritis.

---

### Best Preventive Strategies

1. If you believe you may be at increased family risk for SLE, certainly try to avoid taking the drugs I mentioned above. Ask your doctor to guide you here.
2. Always make sure any physician who cares for you knows of your family risk for lupus before prescribing any drug.
3. Inquire before taking any drug prescribed for you whether or not it has been associated with a lupuslike syndrome.

---

*Triggering Medications and Gout.*   Clinical evidence suggests a number of medications may also increase blood uric acid levels and may promote the development of gouty arthritis in susceptible people. These are the following.

*Thiazide diuretics* are a group of blood pressure lowering medications that promote the elimination of excess fluid through the kidneys. The most commonly used drugs of this class are the generic hydrochlorothiazide (HCTZ) and the brand-name drugs Dyazide and Maxzide. But many so-called combination blood pressure drugs have the HCTZ added to them, such as Inderide (the beta-blocker Inderal or propranolol plus HCTZ), Tenoretic (Ternormin, another beta-blocker plus HCTZ), and others.

*Aspirin,* if taken in low doses such as many older Americans take to reduce the risk of heart attack, can increase uric acid levels, probably by competing with it for removal in the kidney. Many drugs interact with each other in this way. It's as though the kidney were an already crowded subway station, with only so much room for passengers (uric acid molecules) all waiting on the platform to board the next train. If another train comes into the station and unloads another group of passengers demanding to board as well (the aspirin or acetylsalicylic acid molecules), the two groups will have to compete for seats and standing room. Some of both groups will be left behind to wait angrily for the next train. The net effect is that the poor hard-working kidney will be able to remove less uric acid than before, and the body levels will climb.

*Nicotinic acid* is one of the B vitamins that is eliminated in the urine. Taken in small doses, those suggested as the recommended daily allowance, little of the vitamin appears in the urine. At high doses, the excess levels of the vitamin become the second crowded subway train arriving in the kidney.

*Ethambutol* is a drug used in the treatment of tuberculosis. It may cause the level of uric acid to rise, promoting a gouty attack.

*Lead*—although at least in this country and century physicians don't use lead as a medication, sometimes patients become poisoned by lead in paint. Most house paint, nowadays, doesn't contain toxic lead compounds; however, in older homes, the old paint used may contain lead. The problem of buildup of lead from paint exists primarily from children eating the chips from peeling areas such as windowsills. This phenomenon most commonly occurs in economically deprived communities, and an elevation of uric acid would be the least of the evils that could befall a child from this toxic substance.

It is interesting that some historians speculate a high lead content in the fortified wines drunk by our rotund noble ancestors may have accounted, at least in part, for their gouty symptoms.

*Ethanol* is the active ingredient in alcoholic beverages. I have already mentioned its role in promoting gout.

## Trauma

### Osteoarthritis

Traditionally, physicians have attributed the development of the most common form of arthritis—osteoarthritis—to daily wear and tear or chronic trauma. And although the development of joint damage by this mechanism certainly makes sense, several medical studies carried out in the last decade raise some questions. Recent evidence suggests that there may be something, perhaps some sort of genetic predisposition, that causes some people's joints to "wear out" and become arthritic after so many years of day-to-day living and others' to remain supple into late life—even in the face of chronic stresses. That something is as yet unidentified, but perhaps the Human Genome Project will shed some light on its origins. And at this point, the traditional view of osteoarthritis as a wear-and-tear disease still dominates medical thought.

When I was a medical student in the late 1970s we were taught that osteoarthritis struck hardest in the joints of greatest use: in men, who traditionally held most of the heavy manual labor jobs and who spent their youths in competitive, contact sports, the joints usually affected by this arthritis were the large ones used in these endeavors—the hips, knees, shoulders, ankles, and lower back. Women, on the other hand, whom we were told traditionally involved themselves in less strenuous pursuits—housecleaning, needlework, clerical work—suffered small-joint arthritis, more often in their wrists and fingers.

At the time—in the feminist fervor of my early years—I dutifully took those notes to study and learn to pass the next test. But I suspect I also wrote in the margin next to that passage something along the lines of "What a crock!" Anyone who has ever attempted to really clean a house would quickly verify that the joints most traumatized by such chores as vacuuming, mopping, sweeping, and the like are the large ones: the hips, knees, shoulders, ankles, and most definitely, the lower back.

And yet, women do seem to suffer worse arthritis in the small joints of the fingers. Far more of them develop the knobby Heberden's or Bouchard's nodes we discussed in chapter 1. And their development *does* appear to have an inherited basis—the genetic message passing along on a single autosomal chromosome (meaning not one of the sex-determining chromosomes—the X or Y) and via an allele that is dominant in women and recessive in men. The passage of this trait is identical to the simple scheme we covered earlier in the genetics section. And while genetics researchers have yet to uncover the genetic basis for osteoarthritis, inheritance may be strongly at work here, too.

There is little argument, however, that major trauma to joints, such as the kind of bone-shattering injuries sustained in major motor vehicle crashes or serious falls, predisposes *that* joint to early arthritis. Even with adequate, competent orthopedic repair, the damaged bones and supportive joint tissues never truly return to "normal." But rarely would such an injury trigger a bodywide inflammatory arthritis involving joints that had not been damaged by the accident.

An exception to this maxim occurs in psoriatic arthritis. In this condition, trauma to joints does appear to be related to the development of inflammatory arthritis, probably because the immune system cascade is already in full swing—triggered, perhaps, by antigens in the bacteria that infect the skin plaques.

Under normal circumstances, when any joint (or any body tissue, for that matter) sustains an injury, substances released from the damaged tissues signal an immune response. The signals call inflammatory cells into the damaged area to clean up the

---

**Best Preventive Strategies**

1. Avoid repetitive trauma if you can, both in your workplace and in recreation.
2. If you engage in strenuous work, just as in sports, always warm up the joints you will use most and stretch out prior to beginning your day.
3. If you do heavy work for a living, learn and practice—through your employer, a local physical therapist, or college—good body mechanics.
4. Don't ask for injury by trying to be a weekend athlete and a couch potato all week long.
5. Seek medical attention for any injury that doesn't respond in twenty-four hours to ice and immobilization.

mess: to remove dead cells and debris and to repair the injury. If a person suffering from psoriasis seriously injures a joint, activated inflammatory cells in the psoriatic skin plaques—cells capable of responding to the genetic message in which "self" and "nonself" have become confused—migrate to the injured site and stir up trouble. The result? Psoriatic arthritis.

## The Key Is Staying Well

Because this is a book about risk, about being at higher risk for arthritic disease, and about what we can do to *prevent* falling victim to our risk, I have tried thus far to present every possible trigger to the various arthritides and to give you some commonsense advice about avoiding these triggers. Obviously, if in your genetic makeup, you carry the messages that place you at higher risk, you cannot undo that. There is absolutely nothing you can do to change the genetic hand you've been dealt. However, you do have enormous control over how you play your hand and about whether or not you intend to passively become a victim of your risk.

Building and maintaining a healthy, sound body and a strong immune system are integral to staying well. And doing so can do nothing but give you an added advantage over your heritage. In the next several chapters, I want to help you learn how to stay well. I want us to examine the claims that have been made about various foods, vitamins, and minerals in regard to arthritis. Some of them may have no value, but we may want to incorporate others into our blueprint for healthy living. Perhaps by adopting a healthier lifestyle, we can forestall the tipping of that first domino. Perhaps together we can discover a plan to live well and remain well. Let's take a look.

# 4

# Food Facts and Fallacies

I stated earlier that the widespread lack of proper nutrition was likely one of the chief factors behind the explosion of rheumatoid arthritis among the poorer classes of industrial Europe in the nineteenth century. But what would nutritional deficiency have to do with arthritis in the United States today? Don't we live in a land of plenty, where virtually every conceivable kind of food is available most of the year? Yes, we do. And yet, with so much available to us, we still develop chronic diseases. We should all be burgeoning with good health. But, of course, as a nation, we aren't. Why?

Although the vast majority of Americans in the twentieth century *could* eat a nutritionally sound diet, most probably do not. And although the raw materials of healthy eating abound, as a nation, we seem to be eating less of what would keep us fit for a variety of reasons. Some of the reasons may relate to popular dietary misconceptions about what's "good" for us and what's not—myths that will take many years to displace. Other reasons stem from our national obsession with fast food—not just the drive-in restaurant variety, but some of those prepackaged, pre-processed, and ready-in-minutes meals that are higher in price and lower in nutritive value than freshly prepared food. We'll examine some of these "errors of our ways" in this chapter. We'll also take a closer look at foods, vitamins, and minerals from the standpoint of their effect on our basic health, our immune function, and the development of arthritis.

## Food and Arthritis

Since Roman times—and probably before, if we but knew it—physicians have tried to connect what people eat to the development of diseases. Arthritis is no exception, and medical scientists over the years have focused their attention on certain foods, food groups, and particular dietary regimens in an effort to discover such a link. What I wish I could give you is *the* diet that medical science agrees will prevent arthritis, but there is no such agreement. Although the data suggest much and in some areas seem quite reasonable, a strong and certain causative link proves more elusive. However, most of the time the search for a food/arthritis link has revolved around what dietary changes might alleviate the *symptoms* of arthritis that is already established, not what might promote—or prevent—its development in those susceptible to it. That question still begs a conclusive answer.

I can tell you, however, that proper nutrition is crucial to maintaining good health and a strong immunity to disease, and from that standpoint alone, we must view it as one of the cornerstones of a preventive approach to arthritis. And I can tell you as well that research has linked certain dietary factors, such as specific food allergies or sensitivities, with the development of arthritis *in some people.*

And so at the very least, if we do assume a role for nutrition in maintaining a healthy immune system, mustn't we also logically assume that a modern-day "poor" diet—one too often filled with foods devoid of any nutritional value—would after a time debilitate us and impair our ability to resist disease, just as it did in nineteenth-century Europe? And might we not just as reasonably figure that a sound, nutritious diet—one that provided all the raw materials our bodies need to grow and repair, to defend us and protect us—would bolster our resistance to disease and make us healthier?

Yes. Most experts can agree, I think, that proper nutrition tops the list of factors related to building a strong, healthy body and immune system. But then, by extension, can we stipulate that eating "right" could lessen our chances of developing a chronic disease such as arthritis? Perhaps so, but what is "right"? This is no idle question to those of us at risk, so let's take a look at how nutrition relates to arthritis. Are there any specific changes we at risk could make that might give us an edge? Any foods or substances we should avoid or ones, perhaps, that we should eat to make us more resistant to its development? That's the direction I now want to turn in with you, to look over the researchers' shoulders at foods, vitamins, minerals, and supplements as they relate to arthritis. And while we're at it, let's see how these factors may affect our overall health and determine which ones will further our ultimate goal in prevention: to build a strong body and a resistant immune system.

## Sugar

Perhaps chief among the growing reasons Americans eat so poorly is that slowly and insidiously since the turn of the century, a single substance—sugar—has overtaken all other food categories in the American diet. In the last decade or two of the 1800s, Americans consumed an average of about 2 pounds of sugar per person per year. By the late 1980s, we averaged a whopping 127 pounds of sugar (in the form of table sugar, corn syrup, and high-fructose corn syrup) per person per year—a leap in consumption that boggles the mind. Most of you are now thinking: "Well, not me! I hardly add any sugar to my food.

How could I possibly eat that much sugar? Why, a 5-pound bag of sugar will last me six months." And I think that would be true for many of us. But sugar, because of its versatile properties in food production, turns up in almost every processed food on the grocery shelf, from meat entrées to breads to cereals to desserts. And that's where we can sabotage our good nutritional intentions by relying too heavily on those fast, preprocessed foods I spoke of earlier. Look on the labels of almost any packaged food. I will wager that sugar will be listed there; it's everywhere. It's added to soft drinks (literally by the ton, with the major cola companies being the largest consumers of sugar in the world), in candies, cookies, doughnuts, pies, catsup, sauces, puddings, dressings, canned goods, and the list goes on and on. You honestly have to work hard to avoid eating it!

As a group, we well-fed Americans eat more calories per person than the residents of almost any other country, but an ever greater percentage of those calories comes from this substance that contains only calories and is totally lacking in nutritional value. A substance, not only devoid of nutritional value, but actually quite harmful to us, particularly those of us at risk for such chronic diseases as heart disease, diabetes, high blood pressure and—of special interest to you and me—arthritis. Why?

## Sugar and the Aging of Body Tissues

When we eat a food high in sugar—say a soft drink or a candy bar—as we begin to absorb it, our blood sugar rises. When it does, the rise stimulates release of the hormone insulin from the pancreas to bring the level back down. Over time, if we follow a high-sugar meal with a high-sugar snack or cold drink with the next high-sugar meal, and so on, our cells finally become slightly more "resistant" to some of the effects of the insulin, and it becomes a little less potent at returning the blood sugar to normal levels. Finally, a chronically elevated blood sugar *and* insulin results. So, what's that got to do with arthritis?

A chemical bonding occurs between body tissues and the sugar in the fluid that bathes them. This is of particular concern to those at risk for arthritis, because we're talking about tissues such as joint linings, muscle fibers, tendons, cartilage, and ligaments, although this bonding occurs in virtually all other tissues as well. This reaction—called glycosylation—goes on continually and irreversibly in direct proportion to the level of blood sugar, with the bonding altering, and thus aging, the tissues. It's easy to see that the higher the blood sugar on a daily basis, the more this bonding can take place, and the faster the tissues age.

Some speculation also exists among the researchers studying the ways that diet may relate to the aging process in laboratory animals, that once the tissues have undergone this bonding they become more "reactive" and may bond to other substances circulating in the bloodstream. Some research studies also suggest that the changes induced by the bonding could cause the immune system to mistake the now-altered tissues—the glycosylated proteins—as "nonself" and then, as we've seen, the war on them begins.

## Sugar and the Immune System

Our immune system cannot succeed in its ever-vigilant defense of our well-being (when working for us and not against us) unless we maintain it in peak operating form. We must provide it with raw materials in the form of adequate amounts of protein, trace minerals, vitamins, and essential fats through our daily diet to ensure that it can continue its mission. And we must protect it, if we can, from routine exposure to any substances toxic to it. And sugar falls into this category.

Proper immune function depends in part on the presence of certain essential fatty acids that our body must manufacture from certain fats we should get in the diet. In normal healthy young people, that conversion occurs quite readily; however, as we age, or if we're ill, or in the presence of high amounts of dietary sugar, the rate of that conversion falls off. (Some studies show as much as a 50 percent reduction in the bacterial killing power of parts of the immune system in response to a sugar dose.) As a consequence, the immune system suffers, our resistance falls, and we become easier targets for infection.

Certainly, in my role as a general family doctor, I see the clinical evidence for this immune debilitating effect often, especially in children. The children in my practice who must come back to see me time after time with chronic ear infections, throat infections, and bronchitis are more often than not those kids fed diets of sugar-sweetened cereal for breakfast, cupcakes and sugar-sweetened colas with their lunch, and sugary snacks in the afternoon and those who "just won't eat a good dinner," but seem to find room somewhere for the ice cream sundae.

Harken back to your own childhood—twenty-five, thirty, or even forty years ago. How many ear infections do you recall having? Did your mother have to take you to the doctor an average of once a month from the time you were a toddler or preschooler? Mine certainly did not. Except for "well-baby" checkups and immunizations, I rarely visited the doctor's office. What has made the difference?

A part of the answer has to be found in the diet of our children today as compared to the diet of thirty years ago. Although my mother occasionally made a sugary dessert—I used to request her Boston cream pie for my birthday—she never kept quantities of colas, candy, cookies, or sugar-sweetened cereals in the house. We ate some fruit, cheese, milk, or a sandwich if we wanted a snack between meals. Contrast that with today's kids who have an infinitely greater access to sugar, colas, candy, doughnuts and sweet rolls, and sugar-coated cereal, even to the point that this one nutritional zero often comprises the greatest portion of their daily caloric intake. Is it any wonder then that these kids who should be able to easily convert dietary fatty acids to the ones essential for a healthy immune system cannot? Any surprise that they, who should have healthy young immune systems, cannot fend off throat, ear, intestinal, and respiratory infections?

How many of these sugar babies also carry the genetic messages to develop some type of arthritis? Will growing up on a diet that may impair their resistance to infections put them at even higher risk to succumb to their arthritic susceptibility in later life? Perhaps so. And because dietary pollution with sugar doesn't end at puberty, the same case can be made for adults at risk. We carry our sweet tooth with us into adulthood, and with it the tool to debilitate our defenses, and much more.

## Protein

All foods fall into one of three basic food categories—protein, fat, and carbohydrates (sugars and starches). If our diet lacks sugar or starches, our bodies have the remarkable ability to synthesize or manufacture glucose—our blood sugar—from protein. Or we can harvest stored sugar from breaking down our fatty tissues. If what we eat doesn't provide all the fats we need, to a degree we can rearrange the structure of one kind of fatty acid to make another. However, our dietary need for protein is rigid. There are certain required building blocks of body proteins—the essential amino acids—that we must regularly replenish in what we eat, and without which we cannot grow or maintain our body and immune system in a good state of repair.

The human body needs about one-half gram of complete protein (that is, containing all the essential amino acids) per pound of lean body weight each day to be able to maintain its lean mass against the daily wear and tear of living. If the amount is insufficient or the protein incomplete, after a time, the human machine will fail. Among the consequences of protein malnutrition—of particular importance to those of us at risk for arthritis—are alterations in our immune defense that leave us vulnerable to infections that might serve as triggering stimuli and a muscular and ligamentous supportive framework already in poor condition. What can we do?

### Good Sources of Complete Protein

To ensure an adequate daily intake of complete protein, we at risk should choose from a variety of quality protein sources—beef, chicken, turkey, fresh fish, seafood, dairy products, and eggs. The vegetarians among you will be quick to point out that the soybean is also a good source of protein, and you're right. It is not, however, as high a grade of protein as that from animal sources. The gold standard for "perfect protein," the amino acid profile to which all other protein sources must aspire, is egg albumin: the white of the egg.

Red meat, another good source of complete protein, may be especially important because it is an excellent source of both selenium (a trace mineral that research suggests may be important to normal immune function) and of iron, which arthritic patients often have in abnormally low amounts. It is interesting that medical studies show women, who in the childbearing years need extra iron, can absorb and use the iron found in red meat much better than that from other sources, such as iron-fortified vitamins or vegetables or other foods containing equal amounts of iron. There appears to be something (as yet unidentified) in the red meat that enhances the body's ability to scavenge and use the iron. The moral of that story is eat your beef, it's good for you. But you're saying, what about the fat and cholesterol? That's not good for me, is it? Bear with me—I'll get back to that in a minute.

Two other good sources of complete protein, fish and poultry, tend to be leaner and a bit lower in calories (for the weight conscious among you) than beef, and you should try to incorporate these into your diet. Cold-water fish, such as salmon, herring, tuna, and mackerel have the added benefit of containing high amounts of omega-3 fatty acids—the fish oil you've heard so much about—that has shown great promise in alleviating arthritic symptoms. We'll get to the health benefits of such oils in a moment, but first, while we're on the subject of protein, let's turn to the issue of whether the protein in our diet affects the development of gouty arthritis.

**Gout: More Than a Question of Protein Intake?**

What about gout? Hasn't the prevailing medical wisdom in treating gout been to avoid excessive quantities of dietary protein—most notably beef, organ meats, and shellfish? Yes, that's true. The rationale behind giving this advice to patients is that proteins, particularly from those sources I mentioned, break down eventually to form the chemical substance uric acid. And the evolution of gouty arthritis, you will recall from chapter 1, arises from either overproduction of uric acid or insufficient elimination (undersecretion) of it.

Certainly, having less uric acid in the bloodstream seems a reasonable way to go about preventing gouty arthritis attacks and, therefore, advising people at risk for gout to limit or avoid those meat sources would seem a prudent course of action. However, recent research suggests that more may be involved than merely consumption of heavy doses of protein, and here again we meet up with our old enemy, sugar.

Remember I spoke of the portraits of fur-draped noblemen with their round bellies and their gouty toes? Times may have changed, and gout may be a more egalitarian disease, but still today, abdominal obesity and gout go hand in hand. And that's not all. Had we been able to check the blood sugar levels and blood pressure readings on those hefty nobles, I would expect that a great many of them would be high on both counts. I would also expect that were we able to peer into the arteries of their hearts, we would find them choked with atherosclerosis. Because these diseases—obesity, diabetes, high blood pressure, heart disease, and gout—cluster together, recent research (some of it quite new and hot off the research presses) implicates a common factor—insulin—in the evolution of these diseases.

Bring to mind, if you will, one "food" substance that potently drives us to release insulin—sugar. And what did the nobles have access to, because it was an absolute luxury that the poor masses could hardly afford? Sugar. Interestingly, another "food" substance that causes us to release insulin is alcohol, which also happens to be one of the "excesses" that physicians correlate with gout. And so, perhaps a higher protein diet should not be blamed for all the gouty ills of the world.

## Fats and Oils

As I write this, our nation is in the grip of fat-free mania. In keeping with the good old American tradition of giving the public what it wants, the food manufacturers have geared their advertising blitz to ride the fat-free wave. Products of every description, from colas to cookies, from cereal to mayonnaise now noisily proclaim themselves "fat free" or "reduced fat" or "cholesterol free" as though that automatically equates with "healthy." The much more health conscious public of today, thirsty for facts about what will keep them young, well, thin, and free of the scourge of modern society—heart disease—has come to equate *fat* with *bad*, which is not necessarily the case. In truth, we should not view dietary fat as the ultimate villain. Some fat is not only a good thing, but in the case of essential fats, is a *requirement* for good health.

We hear from every corner that our high-fat diet is killing us, and in our quest to remain healthy, we could easily go overboard in removing fats from our diets. We hear, too, that saturated fats especially will send us to early graves. Is this true? The French eat a diet higher in saturated fat than we and have about one-half the amount of heart disease. Most Americans, I would wager, firmly believe that if a blood cholesterol of 180 is good, then one of 140 would be even better. But is it so? Let's take a look and decide on the fat issue. What's our best preventive course?

### Cholesterol

Stand back! We're about to discuss what many of you may look on as the monster of modern life. That nasty fatty substance that plugs up our arteries and kills us with heart attacks. But wait, let's not condemn it so fast. There's much more to the cholesterol issue than you might suppose; for example, to those of us at risk for RA, tracking our blood cholesterol level may serve as a marker to the early development of rheumatoid arthritis. Let's see how.

Cholesterol in our diet comes solely from animal protein—meat, egg yolks, dairy products—because plants neither make nor require cholesterol. Animals (and humans) do. Cholesterol serves a wide range of important functions in the body: it is a major structural component of the walls of our cells, of nerve coverings, and of the brain and is the base molecule from which we make vitally important reproductive (male and female) hormones, natural steroids, bile acids, and vitamin D (this vitamin plays an important role in psoriatic arthritis, as we'll see in a bit). Cholesterol is so critical to human survival that our bodies make it in three separate locations (the liver, the intestine, and the skin). Most of the cholesterol in our blood does not—contrary to what television advertisements would have you believe—come from what we eat. The bulk of it we make ourselves. Just how much of it we manufacture in the liver depends on a production pathway that is sensitive to our old friend, insulin, which you will remember is the hormone we release in response to rises in our blood sugar (i.e., in response to dietary sugars and starches).

Eating a diet that provides sufficient protein and essential fats, and limits sugar and other refined carbohydrates will usually keep the cholesterol level in an optimal 180 to 200 milligram per deciliter (mg/dl) range, because such a diet keeps the reins on insulin secretion and thus limits overproduction of cholesterol. However, in cases of protein/fat malnutrition, or on a very low-fat, high-carbohydrate diet (such as the Pritikin diet, for example) cholesterol levels can fall too low. Very low levels, through mechanisms not entirely understood, may cripple normal immune function (as well as impair the production of sex hormones and vitamin D). A crippled immune system, as we have seen, will leave us more vulnerable to infection and cancer.

Let's get back to arthritis. Studies among the Pima Indians—who as a group have a high incidence of rheumatoid arthritis—have shown that *before* these people develop the signs and symptoms of RA, their cholesterol levels drop significantly. The big question, of course, is do their cholesterol levels drop because they are becoming ill; that is, has the immune system chain reaction already been triggered? Or does the development of the rheumatic disease ensue because the lower cholesterol level leaves the immune system weaker and more vulnerable? Although the answer to that puzzle has yet to be clearly solved, I feel certain that with the huge amounts of money currently being funneled into immune system research (primarily, at present, as it relates to AIDS and not to arthritis), scientists will soon discover answers to many such questions.

The upshot of this discourse on fat and cholesterol is to urge you not to go too far overboard in trying to eliminate all fats and oils from your diet, whatever television ads may say. Remember, some of them play important roles in keeping your body and immune system sound. Let's take a look at yet another group of fats that may assist us in our common goal of preventing arthritis.

### Polyunsaturated Fatty Acids (PUFA)

Certainly, in today's antifat climate, you've heard the phrase *polyunsaturated fats*. They're the ones that are supposed to be so good for you, but why? Do you know what they are? Or what makes a fat *saturated* or *unsaturated*? Unless you have a bent for organic chemistry or biochemistry, probably not, so let me take just a moment to explain.

All fats and oils are made of chains of carbon atoms hooked together by chemical bonds. Each carbon atom has space around it for four such bonds. It can attach to another carbon atom in the chain, leaving three available bonding sites as shown below:

$$-\overset{\displaystyle |}{\underset{\displaystyle |}{C}}-\overset{\displaystyle |}{\underset{\displaystyle |}{C}}-$$

Or it can attach to a carbon atom on either side and have two such sites remaining as the carbon atom in the center does:

$$-\overset{|}{\underset{|}{C}}-\overset{|}{\underset{|}{C}}-\overset{|}{\underset{|}{C}}-$$

Or, it can even doubly bond to its neighbor, using up two bonding sites, but making a less stable attachment (It seems paradoxically so, because you would think that two bonds should be stronger than just one, but such is not the case.):

$$-\overset{|}{C}=\overset{|}{\underset{|}{C}}-\overset{|}{\underset{|}{C}}-$$

When the carbons attached in a chain have all their available bonding sites occupied by hydrogen atoms, they are said to be *saturated* with hydrogen. Fats are usually solid at room temperature (butter, lard, and other animal fats) and have this saturated configuration and are reasonably enough called *saturated fats*.

Oils (usually liquid at room temperature) normally contain one or more of the less-stable double bonds, i.e., some of their carbons are *not* saturated with hydrogen and, therefore, are called *unsaturated fats*. The more of these double bonds the oil contains, the greater the degree of unsaturation, and it is called a *polyunsaturated fat* or *oil*.

Because these double bonds are weaker and more easily broken than the hydrogen-saturated bonds, polyunsaturated fats are not as stable on the grocer's shelf. To make their shelf life longer—or to make the liquids become solids, like margarine—food manufacturers artificially hydrogenate them, i.e., heat them to very high temperatures to force hydrogen into the chain; in effect, they partially saturate them. These oils then become what you've seen on a million food labels: partially hydrogenated corn-safflower-cotton seed-or-whatever-else oil.

Some research has suggested that our bodies may not be as able to break down the bonds thus created by artificial saturation and may, therefore, not derive much benefit from what would have otherwise been a lovely source of essential fats. When we consume these oils, we may be incorporating their altered fat molecules into our cell walls, using them to build our infection-fighting cells and prostaglandins, and relying on what amounts to substandard raw materials. To avoid consuming high quantities of these kinds of oils, while still getting plenty of essential fats, those of us at risk for arthritis might be better served to use cold-pressed oil products—such as olive oil, safflower, or canola oil—that have not been artificially hydrogenated. We might also try to free ourselves from the unreasonable fear of eating "real" butter or animal fat, which our bodies *can* use more readily. Understand that I am not advocating that you should make saturated fat a major component of your daily diet, just that you should not feel that the polyunsaturated, partially hydrogenated oils are particularly a safer or better alternative in our quest to build a stronger immune system.

### What about the Omega Fats?

Another group of PUFAs that has received great attention in arthritis (and heart disease) research circles are the omega-3 and omega-6 fatty acids. (For clarification, the numbers 3 and 6 merely refer to the position of their first double bond in the carbon chain.) These PUFAs gained great popularity in the 1970s and 1980s as the newest "cure" for our national obsession, high cholesterol. The bases for this therapy are studies that showed that traditional Eskimos (who eat a diet very high in omega-3 fatty acids) rarely have heart disease. As could be expected, Americans, ever in the grip of high-cholesterol hoopla, seized for a time on the idea of supplementing their diets with fish oil capsules. However, in recent years, the mania has waned some. The supplements were called fish oil, because the omega-3 fatty acid concentrates in, and is extracted from, the fat of cold-water fish (which is where the Eskimos get it). From this study also came the rationale that eating more fish would promote a healthy heart, although significant quantities of omega-3 fatty acids only occur in the cold-water varieties—tuna, herring, salmon, mackerel, and the like—and not in freshwater species.

Omega-6 fatty acids come from plant sources that are not

even a part of the human diet, but through some clever bio-chemistry, our bodies can create omega-6s by converting omega-3s. This is the conversion that I spoke of earlier that healthy children and young people can easily accomplish, but that is reduced in the presence of a high-sugar diet or illness; the ability to make this conversion declines with age.

These two omega PUFAs are the base molecules from which our body makes several important anti-inflammatory substances (called prostaglandins). Recent fatty acid research has verified their roles in alleviating arthritis symptoms, in boosting healthy immune function, and in lowering insulin levels.

To derive the greatest benefit from the omegas, however, the two need to be present in the proper proportion and must be stabilized to prevent rancidity. The proper proportion is found, interestingly enough, in human breast milk. Once off that food source, which applies to all of us able to read this book, we may need to supplement our diet in these PUFAs in capsule form, much like taking a vitamin supplement. I have listed in the re-source section of this book, what I feel is the best, purest, and most reliable source of omega-3s and omega-6s, and the only such supplement manufactured with the omegas already in the optimal combination. Be sure to check with your own doctor before taking this or any other supplement.

In designing a nutritional plan to optimize our health, there may certainly be a place for supplementing with the omega fatty acids. Maintaining adequate levels of these essential fats may not only help those of us at risk for arthritis to develop healthier immune systems but may also help us to build sounder, stronger tissues.

## Alcohol

The choice of whether or not to consume alcohol is a personal one, and I do not feel it is my place here either to condemn or recommend its use. Certainly, there are those among us who for a variety of reasons (including environmental and/or genetic risk of alcoholism), cannot or should not consume this substance. However, for those readers who do use alcohol, I would like to give you a few facts about it as it relates to arthritis and your all-important immune system.

Alcohol is one of the few substances that is absorbed directly out of the stomach. It exerts noxious effects on the stomach lining and is directly toxic to the pancreas (remember it as the organ that produces, among other things, insulin). Alcohol is a toxic compound and as such must be "detoxified" by the liver (which is our primary defense organ against most poisonous chemical insults). In large doses, or especially if alcohol makes up a substantial portion of daily caloric intake (which, believe it or not, it sometimes does), detoxifying the drug depletes the body of a number of vitamins and trace minerals. Relative deficiencies (particularly of thiamine and magnesium) can result, creating a situation that may cripple our immune function. Aside from these toxic effects, alcohol also stimulates us to release insulin, which as we have seen before, may participate in bringing about attacks of gouty arthritis in those susceptible to it.

Taken in small doses—a glass of wine with dinner or an occasional drink or beer—alcohol will not cause great harm to the vast majority of us, even those at risk for gout. Taken to excess, alcohol can increase risk for those people predisposed to gout and may also play an indirect part in undermining good health in those of us at risk for other kinds of arthritis.

## Caffeine

Along the same lines as alcohol, caffeine causes the release of insulin. For all the same reasons cited above, those of us trying to maintain optimal health should probably avoid heavy doses of caffeine. Once again, moderation should be the watchword: a cup or two of coffee a day, or a caffeinated diet beverage or two would not be out of line.

## Vitamins

Although ideally by eating a healthy diet we should get many of the vitamins and trace minerals necessary for good health, such is not always the case. If our diets lack certain nutrients, in trace amounts, vital biochemical reactions—from wound healing and repair to the clotting of blood to the production of stress hormones—may not operate efficiently. Except for in specific vitamin deficiency states—such as scurvy (vitamin C deficiency), pellagra (niacin deficiency), pernicious anemia (vitamin $B_{12}$ or folate deficiency), or rickets (vitamin D deficiency)—most of us need no more than our proper daily diet and perhaps a single multivitamin and mineral a day to adequately meet the Recommended Dietary Allowances for all vitamins and minerals. (In the resource section, I have included a table listing the RDAs for many vitamins and minerals.)

However, some of these micronutrients have verified or at least possible roles in arthritic disease. Let me take you briefly through a few of them, just so you'll be aware of this information.

### Vitamin D

Vitamin D or, more specifically, *active* vitamin $D_3$, clearly has some potential role at least in the treatment of the skin problems associated with psoriatic arthritis. Studies using preparations containing this vitamin, both taken by mouth as well as rubbed on topically, showed significant reduction in the scaling of the skin. Our bodies normally convert precursors in our skin to active natural vitamin D on exposure to sunlight, perhaps accounting for the improvement of psoriasis by ultraviolet light or sun. Although the possibility is intriguing, I discovered no research that addressed whether this vitamin plays an important role in treating (or preventing) the arthritic symptoms associated with psoriasis. However, because vitamin D does play an important role in maintaining healthy bones (because it is critical to the absorption of calcium from the intestine) it behooves us not to become deficient in it. Remember, though, because vitamin D is a fat-soluble vitamin, which is stored in the liver, you can also get too much of it.

*Dietary Sources*: Nowadays, homogenized milk usually comes fortified with vitamin D. Other good sources are liver, cod liver oil, egg yolks, and fish.

*Other Sources*: In moderation, sunlight allows us to convert vitamin D precursors in our skin to active vitamin D.

### Zinc

The direct role for zinc in arthritic disease is much clearer than for many nutrients. Studies in laboratory animals as well as in humans have shown that deficiencies in this trace mineral depress the immune system—an occurrence those of us at risk would wish to avoid. In fact, if researchers cause a zinc deficiency experimentally in lab animals, they can measure immediate reductions in cell growth and repair functions. And people deficient in zinc become more vulnerable to both infections and cancers. Also, because patients with RA also often show decreased levels of zinc, researchers undertook a study to determine if replacing the mineral would help. The hypothesis here was that patients with RA and psoriatic arthritis might have deranged zinc metabolism and so become deficient. (My question is, does the disease cause the derangement or does the derangement cause the disease? And that issue has not been addressed to my knowledge.) These recent clinical studies did indeed show that *after* rheumatoid arthritis or psoriatic arthritis have developed, the addition of zinc sulfate (220 milligrams taken by mouth three times a day) to the diet lessened joint stiffness, improved mobility, and decreased swelling. Will it help those of us at risk for arthritis in prevention? At least from an immune, growth, and repair standpoint, it can't but help.

*Dietary Sources*: Although present in vegetables, we absorb zinc much better from animal meats, liver, eggs, and seafoods. Certain components of wheat may interfere with absorption of zinc. For this reason, those of us at risk would do well to avoid eating wheat bran, breads, or cereals *at the same time* as zinc-rich foods or supplements.

### Iron

All of you probably connect iron with blood and anemia. Everyone's heard of "iron-poor blood," right? And without doubt, its primary function is in building hemoglobin, the oxygen-carrying protein of red blood cells. When we become deficient in iron (and women, of course, are more likely to do so because of menstrual blood loss) our red blood cells first become a little smaller and paler, because they each contain less hemoglobin. Then we become frankly anemic, meaning that their numbers, too, have fallen off. Less red blood to carry oxygen means less energy, a weaker immune system, and lower resistance to infection.

*Dietary Sources*: Red meat—especially organ meat, such as liver, kidney, heart and spleen—is far and away the best and most readily absorbed source. Next come egg yolks, fish, clams, oysters, nuts, figs and dates, asparagus, and oatmeal. Because vitamin C assists in the absorption of iron, it should ideally be present in the same meal. Contrary to popular belief, spinach is *not* an ideal source of dietary iron, because components in the dark green leafy vegetables can interfere with absorption.

### Vitamin C

As I just mentioned, one of the important roles for this vitamin is to help us absorb iron. But it also has some very interesting immune system–boosting effects. In relation to its role in arthritis, studies of some RA patients have shown low levels of vitamin C in the joint tissues and in the blood. The precise significance of the low levels is unclear at this point, and as yet, studies have failed to prove any certain benefit from its use *after* RA develops. However, because of its immune-enhancing effects and its documented roles in wound healing, growth, and de-

velopment, we should find a place for it in our dietary arma-
mentarium for promoting good general health.

Toxicity from vitamin C is virtually unheard of and although
a daily recommended dose of 60 milligrams should be sufficient
for most cases, proponents of it (such as Linus Pauling) allegedly
take as much as 10,000 milligrams a day without untoward
effects. Our bodies require more vitamin C under stressful conditions—i.e., if we're injured or ill—or to help us detoxify cigarette smoke, if we inhale it.

*Dietary Sources*:    Citrus fruits, tomatoes, potatoes, and leafy
vegetables. The vitamin will not withstand heat and oxidizes
easily, so cooking or prolonged exposure to air will destroy it.


### Copper

Now here is one many of you may have heard about before
in relation to arthritis. Folklore, from as far back as ancient
Greece, has held that wearing a copper bracelet would cure
arthritis or at least relieve its painful symptoms. If without merit,
why has such a remedy persisted for more than 2,000 years?
The answer is it's not totally without merit. Bizzare as it seems,
in some modern-day clinic trials, one group of rheumatoid arthritis patients who wore copper bracelets (the supposition being
that they absorb copper through the skin) experienced more
subjective improvement than another group of RA patients who
were asked to wear identical-appearing aluminum bracelets.
(Neither group knew which kind of bracelet they wore.) Such
results prompted clinical studies using copper taken by mouth,
and the results were quite favorable. The U.S. Food and Drug
Administration (FDA) has restricted the sale of copper salicylate,
apparently to put it under official study as a drug. Thereby, I
suppose, they intend to determine by controlled tests whether
dangerous or unpleasant side effects might arise from its use.

I have just said that some RA patients have improved symptoms by taking copper salts or wearing copper bracelets, and
now, I am going to present you with an interesting paradox.
Sometimes, patients with RA have *high* copper levels, and phy-

sicians prescribe copper chelating drugs (medicines that seek out and scavenge copper, removing it from the body) to treat their disease.

My own father, in fact, who had ferocious inflammation from his RA—even while he took daily potent doses of anti-inflammatory drugs and steroids—finally responded modestly to D-penicillamine, a copper chelating drug. He had for years maintained a sedimentation rate (a blood test used to measure inflammation) of 140 to 150. The normal sedimentation rate value for his age was less than 20. On penicillamine, his sedimentation rate fell to 50 or 60. High for most of us, but great for him.

And so we see that even though too little copper can create problems, so can too much. Where does that leave us in our dietary plan for good health? I would say, because copper deficiency is rare (perhaps because we pick up a good bit of it from copper water pipes) and copper excess is dangerous, on a diet providing any copper, supplementation should never be necessary.

### Selenium

Like vitamin E (discussed below), this mineral functions as an antioxidant to protect our essential fatty acids from alteration and damage. It is, therefore, important to the maintenance of a healthy and normally functioning immune system for all the reasons outlined for vitamin E.

*Dietary Sources*:   Seafood, kidney, liver, and meat. Very little in fruits, vegetables, and grains.

### Vitamin E

This fat-soluble vitamin is an antioxidant, which means that it prevents oxygen from combining with and altering other substances (such as highly unsaturated fatty acids). The higher the intake of PUFAs—which as we have seen may be important to those of us trying to prevent arthritis—the more the need for vitamin E. Although research has not yet established a clear role for this vitamin in the treatment of arthritis, its *potential* role in the immune system may be that it prevents this oxidation process from damaging or changing the unsaturated fatty acids in our cell membranes. Although much less toxic than vitamin D, vitamin E is also a stored vitamin and should not be taken in doses exceeding 1000 IU a day for longer than a few months, except under the direction of a physician.

*Dietary Sources*:   Cold-pressed oils (safflower, sunflower, and olive), cabbage, spinach, and asparagus.


### Vitamin B$_6$

This vitamin is actually three related substances grouped together under one banner. They are required for the efficient and normal metabolism of the building blocks of protein—the amino acids—and our requirement for them increases as protein intake increases. Because a diet adequate in protein is especially important to those of us at risk for arthritis, we'll need to be certain we also get sufficient vitamin B$_6$ so that we can use the protein we eat. Vitamin B$_6$—like all the members of the B-vitamin family—is a water-soluble vitamin and, therefore, is not stored to any great degree. Be cautious about taking it in doses that exceed the RDA, however, because doses as small as 200 milligrams a day have caused problems for some people, ranging from tingling and loss of balance to nerve damage.

*Dietary Sources*:   Beef and pork liver, salmon, herring, brown rice, bananas, and pears. However, because this vitamin is not stable when heated, cooking will destroy it. Because most of us prefer our liver, salmon, and herring cooked and because eating uncooked brown rice is unappealing, that leaves bananas and pears (or multivitamin capsules).


### Pantothenic Acid

A member of the B-vitamin family, this micronutrient plays a key role in energy metabolism pathways in the body. We may require it in higher amounts in times of both physical and emotional stress—times when our immune function may falter a little—because it is essential in the production of natural steroid (or "stress") hormones. To maintain health, particularly immune health, we must not become deficient in pantothenic acid. Absolute daily human requirements have never been determined, but there have also been no reports of toxicity—at any level of intake.

*Dietary Sources:*   Egg yolks, kidney, liver, and unprocessed wheat flour. Although more than half is lost in turning whole wheat flour to white flour, many bakeries add it back in as a "fortifier" in processed cereals and breads.

### Magnesium

This trace mineral plays a critical role in many biochemical reactions important to energy production and to the immune system. We need it, along with calcium, for normal development of our skeletal framework. It is also essential for nerve transmission and for the proper absorption of many of the other vitamins. Deficiency states can and do occur from heavy drinking of alcohol and possibly from high sugar intake.

*Dietary Sources:*   Nuts, seeds, and dark green leafy vegetables.

The human body requires a number of essential nutrients, all of which we need for optimal health, but some of which have less to do directly with arthritis and the immune system than those we have just covered. I do not intend by their exclusion from this dissertation to imply that all the essential nutrients are not important to us. And so, as an addition to those described, let me now simply note that we humans need vitamins A, D, E, K, C, $B_6$, $B_{12}$, thiamine, riboflavin, niacin, folacin, biotin, pantothenic acid, calcium, phosphorous, magnesium, iron, zinc, iodine, selenium, chromium, chloride, potassium, sodium, molybdenum, fluoride, manganese, copper, protein, essential fats, and water.

## The Food Allergy Theory

Recent research has turned up an interesting connection between food and arthritis. It appears that the triggering stimulus to arthritic development for some people may be an allergic hypersensitivity to certain foods or food-related substances. The mechanism by which this occurs is an interesting one. Let's take a look at it.

What happens when people develop allergies to penicillin or dust or dog dander or pollen? Why do some people react so violently to such substances and others do not? The answer lies, once again, in the immune system. Normally, small molecules—such as most allergens—escape notice by the immune system as foreign. And when people susceptible to allergy (like those of us at risk for arthritis who may carry our own specific genetic messages that make us so) come into contact with such a substance, say penicillin, for example, they may not respond to it for years. It is as though the molecule were invisible to the immune system. Then, one day, for some unexplained reason, a body protein may attach to the penicillin molecule and "present" it to the immune system. From that moment onward, the immune system recognizes the penicillin as "nonself" and will mount an attack against it.

In a manner identical to these other forms of allergy, people can develop allergies to some foods or to chemicals in the foods. Their response may be any of a number of typical allergic symptoms, ranging from gastrointestinal distress to nasal congestion to itchy eyes to hives. Or in some cases to the development of joint symptoms—i.e., arthritis.

Eliminating those foods that cause the allergic symptoms from the diet will usually improve the complaints, although it's possible that in the case of arthritis, activation of the silent genetic message may have already occurred. However, we who consider ourselves at risk to developing arthritis are more interested in preventing its occurrence than in alleviating symptoms. Could eliminating potential food allergies or sensitivities benefit us? Possibly, but the jury is still out on that point.

I will speculate, however, that if you come from a family that in addition to arthritis has a strong history of allergies and particularly if you suffer from allergies to environmentals (pollens, dust, animal danders, and molds) yourself, food allergy may be an avenue for you to explore. It could do no harm, and might even prove quite helpful in your goal of maintaining good health, to discuss the possibility of specific food allergies with a specialist and perhaps even undergo blood testing (called RAST testing, discussed below) to see if you react to certain types of food. If you do, it would be prudent to avoid them.

### RAST Testing

Once we respond to an allergen, our bodies manufacture antibodies—called *immunoglobulins*—to attack the allergic invader. These antibodies are specific to that substance, whatever it is, and will only react to it or something very much like it. The antibodies circulate in the bloodstream, and science has recently provided us with a means to identify them. This test, radioallergosorbent testing (RAST), detects these immunoglobulins in a clever way.

If I were your physician and I wanted to check to see if you had an allergy to tomatoes, for example, I would take your serum (the clearish liquid part of your blood) and send it to our allergy reference laboratory. They would take it and place it into a chamber containing a minute amount of tomato antigen. If you were indeed allergic to tomato, there would be specific antibodies against the tomato antigen in your blood, and the two foes would bond together in the chamber. Then the laboratory would add another "tagging" solution that would seek out and affix itself *only* to the antigen-antibody combination. This last step not only "fixes" the combination so it cannot be washed away, it tags it with some substance that a sensitive piece of equipment can detect. Often the tag is a fluorescent one. Then, the lab would wash the chamber, and everything not attached to a tag would go down the drain. If your blood had antibodies to tomato antigen, however, those antibodies would now be trapped so that the machine would be able to "see" them and measure how many of them there are. The more antibodies, i.e., the more positive the test, the potentially more allergic you might be to that antigen. Simple and clever, sure enough, but RAST testing is only one of several ways to detect allergy to foods. And, let me insert a word of caution here: Having antibodies to a particular food antigen does not necessarily mean that the food is causing you problems. Even in the face of a very positive test, an allergist will usually want to confirm the allergy by a food elimination trial, which takes some time. Still, if you think you might be subject to food allergies, a good allergist can help you discover the truth. It is, at least, an avenue to explore in your quest to remain healthy and free of arthritis.

## The Nightshade Family

One particular group of foods—all of which contain the chemical solanine—has been connected to the development of arthritic symptoms in some people and in laboratory animals. The members of this family, called the nightshades, are tomatoes, white potatoes, eggplant, paprika, all peppers except black pepper, and tobacco. For those patients who do exhibit true allergy to the members of this family—perhaps by some complaints other than in joint symptoms at present—excluding these foods could be both beneficial now and perhaps could reduce the likelihood of developing arthritis.

### That Other Nightshade

If you are sensitive to solanine, removing the nightshade family from the diet will do little good if you smoke or use any form of tobacco. Because tobacco also is a member of this family of plants, you would need to exclude it too. Smoking, dipping, or chewing tobacco will continue to expose you—and those around you—to the chemical. I probably do not need to go into the countless dangers of smoking again at this point, but I did want to add that some of you may be frankly allergic or sensitive to it and don't know it. It may at least give you another good reason to quit!

## Strategic Eating—Developing a Dietary Life Plan

Now that we've been through some of the ways that foods can relate to immune function and arthritis, let me suggest a few commonsense nutritional guidelines. You may find it easier to accomplish your dietary goals if you purchase a food counter book that lists the protein, carbohydrate, dietary fiber, and fat content of a wide variety of foods. I have listed a few good ones in the resource chapter.

**Nutritional Guidelines**

Barring any allergy, sensitivity, or intolerance to the following food, here are some suggested guidelines:

- Eliminate or drastically reduce your daily sugar intake. By this I include all items containing significant amounts of corn syrup, honey, high-fructose corn syrup, and molasses—such items as pastries, doughnuts, colas, candies, cookies, cakes, pies, sugar-sweetened cereals, and ice cream.
- Select from among lean cuts of beef, pork, poultry, fresh-water fish, cold-water fish, seafood, eggs, organ meats, and dairy products to consume 55 to 70 grams of high-quality protein a day.
- Select fiber-rich, less starchy vegetables as your dietary staples—foods such as broccoli, asparagus, green beans, cauliflower, dark green leafy vegetables, mushrooms, onions, and cabbage.
- When selecting fruits, choose those with the most fiber and the least sugar—for example, strawberries, raspberries, cantaloupe, and honeydew melon. For the vitamin C content, you might choose a half of a grapefruit or a cup of vitamin

C-enriched sugar-free orange drink with an iron-containing breakfast of eggs or some meat.

- Decrease your consumption of white flour breads. Instead, choose "light," fiber-added breads or oat bran breads when possible.
- Decrease or eliminate your daily intake of starchy junk foods—potato chips, tortilla chips, corn chips, and cheese curls. Try substituting occasional pork rinds (which have no more fat than most chips), popcorn, or sunflower seeds.
- Limit or drastically reduce your daily intake of alcohol and caffeine.
- Increase your intake of omega PUFAs and cold-pressed oils (such as olive and canola oils).
- In addition, you may wish to supplement your daily diet with omega-3 and omega-6 fatty acids and take a multivitamin and mineral complex daily to be certain you meet— or even slightly exceed—the daily minimum requirement for all essential nutrients.

All of these recommendations should, of course, be approved by your own doctor.

# 5

# Preventive Maintenance

The purpose of this book (and all books in the If It Runs in Your Family series) is to give you information about risk assessment of familial diseases—in this case, the arthritides—and, more important, information about what you can do to lessen your risk of their development. As I have said before, the only legitimate reason to determine that you have an increased risk for a particular inherited disease lies in your being able to do something about the disease. Our goal—yours and mine—is prevention of arthritis. And although there can be no guarantees, our best bet in achieving that goal is to make ourselves as strong, fit, and nutritionally sound as we possibly can.

So far, we've looked at the way diet may promote better general health, which in its turn should lessen our chances of succumbing to our genetic heritage. And conversely, we've seen that poor nutrition can contribute to a deterioration of our health and immunity, which may open a window of vulnerability to the arthritis stimulators from the germ world, and thus increase our risk.

Without doubt, nutritional soundness is of critical importance to good health. However, we must not forget that it is only a part of a comprehensive life plan. In addition, we at risk must endeavor to become physically sound through regular, reasonable exercise, and to maintain that fitness throughout our lives. Although I do not want to curb your zeal to accomplish that goal, I would like to insert a word of caution at this point: If at present you would put yourself in the "out-of-shape" category, please exercise prudence before you exercise your body. Get a complete medical checkup if you've not had one recently, and tell your doctor what kind of exercise you're planning to begin. With your personal physician, make certain there are no overriding health reasons for you not to embark on a program of fitness and conditioning. Then once you've received your clean bill of health, get going.

When you do begin your journey to fitness, resist the impulse—a quite natural one to many of us and I include myself here—to try to repair a decade of inactivity in a few weeks. Don't try to do too much too soon. Those of us in the thirty-something age group who possess a competitive streak—and we know who we are—easily fall victim to this trap.

It would shame me to count how many times I have decided over the last ten years to get myself back into shape. (Although I've never really let myself get *too far* out of condition, I'm most assuredly not and very likely will never be the athlete I was in my youth.) Still, there have been many ups and downs, false starts, and failures to keep faith with my good intentions over the last twenty years. And the scenario was usually the same.

First, I would sign up for a "special" membership in a health club or workout facility—you know the ones, ten weeks for $30, or some such thing. Next, I would drag out my sweatpants and leotards. Then on my arrival for the first aerobics class at the club—fully aware that I had not participated in an intensive workout for, say, one or two years—I would proceed to doggedly keep up with the eighteen-year-old teeny-bopper leader who earlier that morning was poured into her fluorescent spandex outfit. I would push myself to keep going as she popped her gum and urged me forth to do just "four more . . . three more . . . two more . . . " Ignoring the sweat pouring down my beet red face, oblivious to the aching in my chest and legs, heedless of my gasping breath, I pushed onward, determined to keep up with her as though I, too, were still a well-conditioned eighteen-year-old who could teach aerobics five days a week to out-of-shape adults without ever breaking a good sweat. And I relied on my competitive spirit to carry me along enough to at least keep pace and save face at the moment, only to end up collapsed in an exhausted pile later at home. Sometimes, I would hang in for a few months and see my conditioning improve somewhat, but soon one excuse and then another would prevent me from attending class. Before long, my hard-won fitness would escape me again, and there would go my good intentions down the drain. Other times, I would so traumatize my muscles and ache so profoundly that I crept about the clinic for days afterward, grousing loudly about how miserable I was and vowing never to be so foolish again. Let me tell you from years of doing it the wrong way, that's *not* how to go about it!

Rest assured that no matter what your current level of conditioning, you will be better served to attain your fitness in progressive, tiny increments than to injure yourself by deciding to get back into shape by the end of the week. I urge you to avoid injury, not only because it will slow your continuing progress toward fitness, but also because the injury may actually stimulate the development of certain types of arthritis.

When you damage a joint, it and its surrounding tissues release inflammatory chemicals into the bloodstream that function to draw specialized immune white blood cells to the area of injury to clean up the debris. However, particularly in the case of psoriatic arthritis, the trauma to a joint may summon sensitized or activated immune white blood cells from the nearby inflamed skin to the injured area. Some researchers suggest that this phenomenon—stimulation of the development of psoriatic arthritis by joint trauma—is the mechanism at work in patients with susceptibility to this disease. And clinical experience has verified that in patients with gouty arthritis, trauma to joints or even overuse of joints can prompt an attack. Clearly in these kinds of arthritis, overzealous pursuit of fitness may cause harm, and although with less medical certainty, the potential for exercise injury to trigger arthritic symptoms may exist for the other arthritides as well.

And so I implore you to obey the first precept of any medical regimen: First do no harm. Approach exercise as you would a prescription drug or other therapeutic recommendation, by following the guidelines I will give you and your own doctor's admonitions. Consider this: If you came to me complaining about a sore throat, and I gave you a prescription for penicillin to be taken one tablet four times every day for ten days, you would never even consider taking all forty tablets at once on the first day. Like prescription medications, exercise does *not* fall into the "if a little is good, a lot is better" category. Your prescription for health-promoting conditioning is as follows:

1. Begin slowly at a level you can handle today.
2. Increase gradually according to a planned regimen.
3. Once conditioned, strive to maintain what you've gained.

## What Kind of Exercise Is Best?

Should you jog? Swim? Bike? Walk? Dance? Play tennis? How should you go about planning a lifelong program of exercise that suits your lifestyle, improves your conditioning, helps control your weight, and keeps your muscles and joints supple and resilient? Sounds like a pretty tall order, doesn't it? How much of what kind of exercise is best for you? To answer these questions, let me first divide exercise into two broad categories: endurance exercise and static exercise. What's the difference between the two?

Endurance exercises are those that promote heart and lung fitness: jogging, biking, swimming, walking, and stair stepping. Static exercises—like weight lifting—develop strength, power, and resilience in the musculoskeletal system. There is a good deal of overlap between the two, as I am sure you can see, but for the most part, we improve our cardiopulmonary conditioning best with endurance work and our muscle tone best with static exercises.

For you and me—the segment of the population at higher risk for arthritis—which form is best? Actually, both. We derive important benefits by improving endurance as well as tone, and so we should develop a plan of regular exercise that incorporates some of each. But depending on our present level of conditioning, that plan may be radically different for each of us. Once again, our goals must be:

- DO NO HARM.
- BEGIN SLOWLY.
- INCREASE GRADUALLY.
- STAY AEROBIC.

You may now be saying, "Stay aerobic! But I thought she said not to try to keep up with an aerobics workout at the outset." That's true, I did say that. However, that brings me to my next point, which is that *aerobic* does not mean bouncing willy-nilly in neon spandex. Aerobic means *in the presence of oxygen*. In its true sense as applied to conditioning, aerobic means that during exercise we do not ask our muscles to work beyond their capacity to extract oxygen from the blood. Let's explore that idea a little more deeply.

### Aerobic Muscle Work

Every time we use a muscle for any purpose, the energy needed for that muscle to function properly is the result of a complicated series of biochemical events in which oxygen plays a key role. We all know that a flame cannot continue to burn without oxygen, and in much the same way, our muscles require oxygen to "burn" their fuel efficiently to produce the energy needed for them to work. As long as the muscle fibers receive plenty of oxygen, they can produce energy quickly and efficiently along the *aerobic pathway*, which burns fat and glycogen (a storage form of glucose) as fuel. In the absence of sufficient oxygen, the muscle fibers turn to a second, less-efficient energy production means, the *anaerobic pathway*, in which they burn blood glucose for fuel. A by-product of oxygenless glucose burning is lactic acid, which builds up in the muscle tissue and causes pain. We rid our body of this excess lactic acid by breaking it down into carbon dioxide, which we exhale through our lungs. The more lactic acid our muscles build up, the more carbon dioxide we produce, the faster and more deeply we must breathe to keep pace.

Now I want you to pretend to exercise. As you begin, your lungs take in a breath and extract the oxygen from the air and pass it into your bloodstream where your red blood cells carry it along to the muscles and other tissues. Unless you suffer from severe lung disease, such as emphysema or severe asthma, your lungs can usually keep up with your exercise demands. (I can hear some of you thinking: "Wait a minute. The first thing that happens to me when I exercise is that I puff and pant. My lungs give out right away." But actually, your lungs are not the problem, and I'll tell you why in a moment.) And, likewise, in the absence of severe heart disease, your heart can pump the oxygenated blood around to the muscles quickly enough to keep them well supplied. So your lack of cardiopulmonary endurance really does not lie with your heart or your lungs. Then where?

The next step in the scheme is for your muscles to harvest the oxygen from the blood as it passes through them. Unless you are in good aerobic condition, here is where the bottleneck occurs. If you exercise beyond the ability of your muscles to remove oxygen from the bloodstream, the muscles must turn to the *anaerobic pathway* for fuel to continue your work. The more strenuous the demands you make on them, the more quickly they will reach the point of their maximum ability to extract oxygen, and the more quickly they must turn to anaerobic burning of blood glucose.

But, of course, you don't stop and rest then, because the teen-ager in the hot pink spandex is still shouting "just four more." And so you continue the demand, and the by-product, lactic acid, builds up in your muscles. You begin to "feel the burn" Jane Fonda told you about. The higher the levels build, the more lactic acid you must break down to form carbon dioxide to rid yourself of the excess, the faster and more deeply you must breathe, and *voilà*, you're panting like a lizard. Not because your lungs couldn't keep up. Not because your heart is weak. But because your muscles are not yet up to the task of oxygen extraction at that level. Improving their ability to do this is the goal of endurance exercise.

To prevent injuring yourself along the way, begin at whatever level of low-impact aerobic dancing, walking, swimming, biking, or stair climbing that you can tolerate. And by tolerate, I mean begin at the level at which you maintain your pulse rate at about 65 percent of your maximum rate (I'll tell you how to calculate this next). This should ensure that you don't overdo it at the beginning and that you remain in an aerobic state during the work. Remember, the amount of exercise it will take to keep you exercising aerobically will most likely be vastly less than what Miss Spandex of America requires—at least in the begin-ning—so don't fall into my trap and try to keep pace with her from the start. If you do, your muscles will most likely be forced into the anaerobic pathway very soon, they will hurt, you will hurt, you will hate exercise, and your zeal will have defeated the entire purpose.

### The Training Effect

To achieve the maximum conditioning benefit from endurance exercise of any kind, you should perform it initially at a level that keeps your pulse at about 65 percent of its maximum and gradually increase to 75 percent or even 80 percent once your conditioning improves enough. But what's the maximum? How do you go about figuring that? One quick-and-simple way to make a rough estimation is to subtract your age from 220. For example, if you are thirty-two years old: $220 - 32 = 188$ beats per minute as a maximum heart rate. To find your initial pulse level for aerobic exercise, take your maximum (in this example, 188 beats) and multiply it by 0.65 as follows: $188 \times 0.65 = 122$ beats per minute.

So when you first begin to walk, stair climb, swim, or do low-impact aerobics, you should measure your pulse rate after a few minutes and again at regular intervals throughout your exercise program. It should not exceed the 65 percent figure. If it does, slow down—whatever Miss Spandex might say! As you become comfortable exercising for twenty minutes at that level—and take your time getting comfortable—increase to 70 percent of maximum (in our example, $188 \times 0.70$ or about 131 beats per minute) for twenty to twenty-five minutes. Then ease on up to a thirty-minute workout if you like, or move up to 75 percent of maximum. You can slowly increase either the time you exercise or the intensity of the workout, but do so according to a plan.

During the training phase, you should try to exercise four or five times a week to improve your conditioning continually, you should never exercise more than two days in a row, and you should never skip exercising for more than two days. I have included an example of what your training and conditioning exercise schedule might look like on page 158.

## Which Kind of Endurance Exercise Should You Try?

Choose whatever kind of endurance exercise you believe that you will enjoy and be able to do, given your abilities, access to facilities, and climate. Let's examine the pros and cons of several of these.

### Jogging

Americans have gone jogging crazy in recent years. Some of you may even be runners. The burning question for those of us at risk is this: will the daily wear and tear on weight-bearing joints during jogging harm the joints? If you've been jogging regularly since your teens and twenties and have not been subject to joint pain, tendinitis, bursitis, and the like, the answer for you is probably no, particularly if you are male.

However, unless you have done so all along, and especially if you are over thirty-five, I would advise against jogging simply because the aerobic conditioning benefits are no greater than for brisk walking, but the impact on joints could be much worse. In fact, according to Dr. Rene Cailliet, a specialist in physical medicine and rehabilitation at the University of Southern California Medical School, jogging increases the forces of weight bearing on the hips, knees, ankles, and feet dramatically. Compared to standing still, walking increases the weight-bearing load on these joints by four times, jogging increases it by nine. Or to put it a little differently, each time your foot hits the ground during jogging, you inflict more than twice the compressive jolt on the cartilage surface of your joints and on the tendons and ligaments that support the joints than you would during walking. With aging—and Dr. Cailliet pinpoints thirty-five years old as the breakpoint—the cushioning cartilage surfaces that cover our joints become less resilient, less able to absorb the shock of running. Instituting a running program after the age of thirty-five when the cartilage surfaces have lost some of their suppleness may increase the risk of microfractures (microscopic shattering or cracking of the cartilage). These tiny breaks may in turn stimulate an inflammatory response in the joint and increase the risk to develop arthritis in the joint.

Although, as I mentioned earlier, in the studies evaluating the role of jogging trauma and the development of osteoarthritis, researchers *did not* find conclusive evidence of an increase in osteoarthritis of the knees and ankles among male joggers, the same was not true for female joggers, who did display some increase. And although there was no apparent increase in knee arthritis among long-distance runners who continued to jog into advanced age, we must bear in mind the possibility that those runners whose knees began to bother them somewhat early on in their running careers may have given up the sport before they developed frank osteoarthritis. And those who were not susceptible to it continued to run. The role of repetitive trauma in the development of osteoarthritis, also finds some support, in the studies that show an increased incidence of arthritis in the dominant hand—i.e., in the right hand of right-handed people—that naturally does more of the work and receives more of the day-to-day trauma.

And so where does that leave us in regard to the prudence of jogging? Simply this, I think, if you've been running for years and have suffered no consequences from it, by all means, run on. If you are female, over thirty-five, and have never really run regularly, I would advise you to choose another form of endurance exercise less traumatic to your joints. Let's look at a few alternatives.

### Biking

A slightly more expensive sport to cultivate than running because of the equipment involved, biking offers a means to engage in long-distance aerobic activity without the weight-bearing stress on knees, hips, ankles, and feet. Outdoor biking is not without risk of injury, even among cycling aficionados. In my medical practice, I've taken care of quite a few expert bikers who were bruised, battered, broken, and abraded from nose to toes when their equipment failed or they were forced off the road by a motorist.

A safer biking alternative might be indoor exercycling, even though the scenery isn't quite as good. Exercise bikes also have the advantage of predictable intensity—i.e., you just set the resistance to what you can pump, set a timer or watch the clock for the length of your workout, and measure your pulse from time to time. (And not have to fear you're going to run off the road when you do it.)

For most of us at risk for arthritis, biking (indoors or out) can be a great way to stay fit. However, it is the very worst sport to choose for those of you at increased risk for AS. The deforming curvature that we associate with ankylosing spondylitis, or arthritis of the spine, will be promoted by the hunched-over biking posture. People with AS—and I will extend that to include those at risk for the disease as well—must strive every waking minute to maintain erect posture. They must try to avoid any activity that requires them to maintain a stooping or bent neck posture, and biking falls into this category. Because the earliest changes of AS begin in young men in their teens to early twenties, this advice is especially important for them. What endurance sport would be better for them?

### Stair Climbing

The recent popularity of the stair climbing or stepping machine changed the prospect of exercise, at least for me. Prior to discovering the fitness stepper, I walked for exercise, which I enjoy and still do when the weather is good—which it is about half the time. However, in Arkansas, it's usually blazing hot in late July and August and miserably humid, and tends toward the cold and wet in the winter. And so I would find myself filled with resolve and easily able to take my daily constitutional in the glory of spring mornings, early summer evenings, and crisp fall afternoons. But the rest of the time, I had to fight my own sloth, and sloth often won. To rescue me from myself, my husband and kids bought me a fitness stepper last Christmas. I had looked at them in the stores, tried a few steps on them a time or two. The stepper works the same large muscle groups used in biking, but without the saddle sores.

I donned my sweatsuit Christmas morning and set off for a good step. I stopped, exhausted, heaving for air, and practically unable to lift my legs, after three minutes and four seconds. That sounds like a pretty poor excuse for aerobic conditioning, I'll admit, but I've heard of people who can't even make it past one minute the first time. Others have likened it to the exertion of running . . . uphill. So, there I began at three minutes and four seconds, determined not to give up this time and not to overdo it either.

I laid out a plan to increase my stepping time *very* slowly, going up in mere fifteen second increments each time. So small an increase that I could hardly notice the difference, but by April I was effortlessly stepping off sixteen or seventeen minutes. No sweat. And then I began to increase the resistance on the stepper to make the workout a little more difficult. Again in small doses, designed to let my body's condition gradually improve to keep pace with the increasing demands I was putting on it.

Fitness stepping gives you an excellent aerobic workout, provided you begin at a level that you can manage without undue stress, whatever that may be—even if it's a half a minute to begin with. To derive metabolic, cardiovascular, and health benefits from any aerobic workout, you should strive to maintain the exertion continually for fifteen minutes at a minimum, but there is no law that says you can't work up to that. Other advantages of a stepper workout are that it can be done regardless of weather, and it works the same large muscle groups as biking, but does not require stooping the back and neck, an important feature for those at risk for AS. One drawback is that you can't easily take a stepper with you when you travel. You can, however, pack your walking shoes and either hit the road or climb the actual stairs at a hotel.

### Swimming

In the semiweightlessness of water, you can get a better heart and lung workout for less joint trauma by swimming than any other endurance sport. The main problem for many people will be access to a swimming pool. However, the plethora of community pools—at YMCAs, YWCAs, and health clubs and in apartment and condominium complexes—should provide more people with a place to swim.

Swimming—especially the backstroke—may also be an excellent aerobic choice for the person at risk for AS. That stroke in particular will encourage an upright posture, strengthen the back muscles to resist the forward bend, and keep the shoulder girdle and back supple and mobile.

Many of the YWCAs and YMCAs around the country offer water exercise classes for people with arthritis in conjunction with the Arthritis Foundation. Although these programs are not designed for the "at risk" population, some of you no doubt have family members suffering from arthritis who might benefit from gentle, joint-sparing exercise offered through this program. (After all, you wouldn't consider yourself at risk if you didn't have someone in your family with arthritis, would you?) I have listed information about these Y programs in Chapter 9.

### Aerobic Dancing

Either low-impact or no-impact aerobic dancing offers an excellent cardiopulmonary and muscular endurance workout. However, bear in mind what I said before, if you tend to be competitive by nature and have not remained in excellent aerobic condition since your teens, don't trot out there the first day of class and do yourself in. Take it slowly and easily. Exercise only intensely enough to drive your pulse to 65 percent of maximum at the outset. If the class is designed to continue for thirty minutes or forty-five minutes and you begin to feel the strain, stop dancing, cool off by gently moving your legs and arms, stretch out a bit, and call it a day.

Because of the increased stress on joints and female pelvic organs (uterus, fallopian tubes, ovaries, and bladder) during high-impact aerobic workouts, I would advise against your initiating such a program. If you've been an avid high-impact dancer for years, I would still recommend the low-impact variety for those of you at risk for arthritic disease. There's just no sense in tempting fate, and the heart, lung, and muscle benefits are no better.

### Walking

And now, I come to my all-time favorite endurance exercise, walking (the previously cited glories of fitness stepping notwithstanding). If I lived in an area with routinely good weather, moderate temperatures, and low humidity, I would walk every day. I might walk every*where*. In a good, supportive, comfortable pair of shoes, I think I could walk to China and back. And therein lies the beauty of walking: you can do it anywhere, at home or on the road, it requires little or no equipment, no membership in a health club, and it can be done with a friend, in a group, or all alone. It doesn't even require any special athletic prowess, grace, or finesse. It's an egalitarian endurance sport virtually everyone can participate in. And it's an excellent choice for those of us at risk for arthritis who wish to improve our cardiopulmonary conditioning, muscle tone, our sense of general health and well-being, and do it without overly stressing our weight-bearing joints.

The one important factor to happy walking is good shoes. Without them, walking can be a misery instead of a joy. New Yorkers all know this, but then, they have to, because they live in a city that demands an enormous amount of daily walking. It doesn't take many twenty-block jaunts down Fifth Avenue in shoes cut for style and not comfort to make you join them in donning comfortable walking shoes and throwing your good shoes into your bag.

And so, I encourage you to consider walking. And if you choose to make it your conditioning sport, approach it precisely as I did my fitness stepper. Begin at a pace you can maintain for fifteen minutes and then each day try to increase the distance you cover in that length of time gradually. Then gradually increase the length of time as well. If at first (as I was on the stepper) you simply cannot walk at any pace for fifteen minutes, walk five, or four, or three minutes and four seconds. Begin where you can, set out a schedule to increase your time and distance in small doses, and stick to it. Shoot for a twenty- to thirty-minute walk at 65 percent maximum pulse, then 70 percent, then 75 percent. End your walk—and any of the endurance exercises—with a slower pace over five or ten minutes to cool down. And remember, I've included a sample schedule sheet on page 158 to help you get started.

Whatever the endurance exercise you choose, remember the guiding precept of medicine: First do no harm. If you can follow that premise, you will be able to do a lot of good for your physical and emotional health.

## Static Exercises

I said before that we improve our muscle tone, joint suppleness, strength, and power through static exercises such as weight lifting. By this, I'm not advocating that all of you become body-builders with bulging muscles. Far from it. Rather, for those of you so inclined, I'd recommend a very conservative program of weight training. To undertake such a program, naturally, you have to have weights, access to weights, or access to a health club. Some of you may have none of the above, and may have little or no desire to engage in this activity. And that is fine. However, approached properly, I think you could reap some health benefits, and so I mention it. For those of you who do wish to participate in weight training, here are some general guidelines. Be certain you've checked with your personal physician and that there is no reason you should not engage in lifting before you begin. Be certain to tell him or her what you have in mind. Your doctor may even be able to recommend a reputable gym or health club in your area. If you've never lifted before, you would be safer beginning in this kind of an organized setting where you can be guided along by a trainer. In any case, my advice is this:

1.  Regardless of what anyone else tells you, it's not "No pain, no gain!" For those of us at risk for arthritis, it's "Feel pain, no gain!" If you feel pain, you're defeating your purpose. After all, your objective here is not to hurt your muscles or joints, it's to rejuvenate them, to make them supple, to keep them strong.
2.  Begin at a weight you can *easily* lift properly—that means with a smooth, fluid motion. Not grunting, jerking, stretching, straining, and arching your back. Whatever you do, do *not* arch your back. It was not designed to lift—your legs or arms should

do that job. No matter how light the weight—and my gentlemen readers, I speak to you mostly here—don't try to lift more than you can lift simply because someone else at the machine next to you is lifting more.

3. Repeat that lifting exercise at that weight eight times or until you cannot do it properly, whichever is less. If it's twice, so be it! Then move on to work another area of the body.

4. Become comfortable performing the lifting exercise at that weight for three sets of eight repetitions each before you move to a higher weight. And when you do, do it *slowly*, in the smallest increment you can.

5. If it hurts, stop it. You may either be lifting improperly or lifting too much. In either event, stop the lifting until you determine what you're doing wrong.

6. Do not weight train more than three days a week as a maximum level, and always allow a day or two to recover before lifting again.


Be careful, and good luck.

# 6

# The Tools of Diagnosis

In your quest to deliniate as accurate a family portrait for arthritic disease as you can, you may have to do a little investigative reporting of sorts. You may, as I mentioned in chapter 2, have to assemble clues about the arthritic history of family members who are dead, unreachable, or even maybe uncooperative. To do this, it may help if you have a grasp on the procedures that we physicians use to unravel the mysteries of joint disorders. Some of the diagnostic tests that physicians use to evaluate patients with arthritis are described next. I think if you are familiar with them, the criteria for diagnosis will be more meaningful.

## Blood Tests

The arthritis panel is a group of blood tests that encompasses the major markers for common arthritic diseases. In our laboratory, it includes the following tests.

*RA Titre.* This blood test is designed to detect the presence of an antibody that years ago was named the "rheumatoid factor." Although this antibody is seen with other diseases as well, it is present in 90 percent of patients with RA. If it is present in the blood, and elevated above a certain level, we say that the blood is RA positive, or rheumatoid factor positive, but this test alone does not make the diagnosis of RA.

*ESR.* The erythrocyte (red blood cell) sedimentation rate test, which was mentioned in chapter 4, relies on the fact that in an inflamed or infected state, the red blood cells become coated by immune proteins, become heavier, and will, therefore, settle in a measuring tube faster. The faster their rate of settling, the higher the sedimentation rate. The ESR is a nonspecific test, which means that if it's elevated, it doesn't tell you what's causing the high reading; it just indicates that *something* is. Physicians rely on it as an excellent marker for the presence of inflammation or infection; it's an even better test to judge the patient's response to treatment. If the ESR is high, it's important to determine why. If it is in the normal range, a serious illness that causes whole-body inflammation is a less likely possibility.

*Uric Acid.* This test measures the blood level of the chemical that we associate with gouty arthritis. Although the correlation is not a perfect one, because people with gouty attacks do not always have dramatically increased blood levels of uric acid, it is still a useful means to pick out those people who do exhibit high levels and are likely to be at increased risk for gout. It also gives physicians a way to gauge the response to treatment by following the declining blood level of the uric acid.

*Antinuclear Antibodies (ANA).* This test, one of several used to diagnose systemic lupus (SLE), detects special antibodies to proteins found in the nuclei of our bodies' cells. Ninety-five percent of patients with SLE will have these antibodies in their blood, often in very high levels. In recent years, the testing has been refined to detect even more specific antibodies to special parts of the genetic material in the nucleus.

*The "LE Prep."* This test was once the standard in the diagnosis of systemic lupus, but with the advent of high-tech immunofluorescence tests, we no longer rely on it as much. However, some of you may be looking into a relative's medical history that is more than ten years old and, consequently, you may come across mention of the LE cell preparation. Here's a brief description: A medical technician takes a fresh drop of the patient's blood, spreads it in a thin smear across a glass microscope slide, and stains it with special stains. The technician can then search the microscopic slide to detect "LE cells," which are nothing more than clumps of nuclear (genetic) material bound to antibodies that have a characteristic appearance. The LE test is a much cruder variant of the immunofluorescent antibody tests in use today, such as the ANA test mentioned already.

## Joint Aspiration

When arthritic joints swell, the excess joint fluid that accumulates in them can provide valuable clues to the cause. Physicians may draw off some of this fluid with a hypodermic needle and a syringe to examine its characteristics. For example, in gouty arthritis, crystals of uric acid that form in the fluid are visible when examined under a special kind of microscope lens. The fluid from a rheumatoid arthritic joint will display other characteristics, such as poor ability to clot and a high number of inflammatory white blood cells.

## X Rays

Although arthritic changes in bones and joints detectable on X ray usually do not occur until the arthritis is well established, physicians may turn to the use of X-ray pictures to aid in diagnosis. In the early stages of some arthritic diseases, X rays may help to prove what the disease is *not* more than to clinch an arthritic diagnosis. Although a few changes occur in the hands of rheumatoid arthritis patients within a few months of the onset of their joint symptoms and subtle changes may show up in the sacroiliac joints (the pelvic joints that lie on either side of the lower back below the waist) early in the course of the spondylopathies, most X-ray changes take time to develop.

Finally, however, for those of us at risk, there are many characteristic changes that may crop up in medical histories of our relatives that would help point to one or another of the various arthritides. Some of the more common changes, detectable through the use of X ray, are the following.

*Periarticular Thinning.* Thinning of the calcium in the bone ends near the joints often occurs in RA. This gives these areas a darker, washed-out (or *radiolucent* in medical parlance) appearance. This is the change that may occur very early in the course of RA, especially in the hands.

*Osteophyte (Bone Spur) Formation.* These bony outgrowths occur at the edges of any joint, but are often found on the fingers of patients with osteoarthritis (i.e., the Heberden's or Bouchard's nodes we spoke of in chapter 1).

*Spondylitis.* This term relates to the bony bridges that fuse and join the bones of the spine together in the spondylopathies: AS, psoriatic arthritis, ulcerative colitis, and Crohn's disease.

*Erosions.* These changes are seen in the joints of patients with RA and are caused by the active pannus—the growing, swollen joint lining that burrows into surrounding bone, tendon, and other soft tissues, eroding and destroying them.

These diagnostic tools represent only a fraction of the medical tests used in determining what kind of arthritis a patient may have. But these few are among the first tests that physicians will order to screen for arthritis and the ones you will most likely come across in your search.

## Diagnostic Criteria for the Arthritides

You will recall that I mentioned some of the classic, or typical, signs and symptoms of the various inherited arthritides in chap-

ter 1 when I began to ask you to evaluate your own family risk
for these diseases. If you must make an educated guess or a
presumptive arthritic diagnosis for family members who are no
longer living or otherwise not available to you, I would now
like to provide some information that will help make your de-
tective work a little easier. You may also want to enlist the help
of your personal physician to interpret your findings.

And so, here are the clinical criteria that physicians use to
determine which of the arthritides a patient has. I have adapted
these listings from the Arthritis Foundation's *Primer on Rheumatic Diseases* (1988) and from the book *Scientific American
Medicine* (1988).

Remember that even in experienced medical hands, nailing
down the culprit that is causing an arthritic syndrome takes time
and effort. Sometimes, it may take a number of years for a patient
to develop enough of the criteria for a physician to make a
definite diagnosis. Because there is a fair amount of medical
jargon sprinkled throughout these criteria as they are written
(after all, they were written for physicians who speak that slang),
I've tried to eliminate as much of it as was possible. Where
impossible, I'll try to act as your interpreter.

### Criteria for Classification of Rheumatoid Arthritis
• Diagnosis of *Classic RA* requires seven of the following
criteria. (My poor father had them all, and so during my training,
I had a living example of each of them.) The symptoms of criteria
one through five must be present continuously for at least six
weeks. Any one feature among those listed under exclusions
(pages 127–128) will eliminate RA as a possibility.


1. Morning stiffness.
2. Physician-observed pain on motion or tenderness of one
   or more joints.
3. Physician-observed swelling in at least one joint caused

by soft tissue thickening or fluid on the joint, and not by bony nodules or spurs.

4. Physician-observed soft-tissue or fluid swelling in another joint before three months' time has elapsed.

5. Physician-observed simultaneous swelling of *both* of a pair of joints—i.e., both wrists, both knees, proximal interphalangeal (PIP) joints (the middle knuckle) on both hands, etc.

6. Physician-observed subcutaneous nodules. (Note: These are soft, rounded, cystlike lumps that arise over bony points such as along the bottom of the arm near the elbow or next to joints. These are not the same as "ganglion cysts" about which you may have heard, which are out-pouchings of joint lining filled with fluid, often seen on the wrist.)

7. X-ray changes typical of RA (which must include thinning of the calcium in the areas of bone next to the joints).

8. A positive blood test for RA (the test for the rheumatoid factor).

9. Poor mucin (a joint fluid protein) precipitate from joint fluid. (Note: In this test for RA, the physician draws off some of the fluid swelling in the joint with a needle and syringe and places it in a tube with a weak acetic acid—vinegar and water—solution. In normal joint fluid certain protein components (mucin) will form a clot, much as blood does. The fluid from the rheumatoid joint, however, doesn't make a nice firm clot, but instead shreds, making the fluid cloudy. Examined by other laboratory means, the joint fluid also will contain many inflammatory white blood cells and will not contain any of the crystals seen in gouty arthritis.)

10. Characteristic changes in the joint-lining tissue when examined under the microscope. For this test, a pathologist examines microscopic slides of specimens of the joint-lining tissue, which have been surgically removed. The precise nature of these changes wouldn't

even interest a nonpathologist physician, and so I will spare you the details.

11. Characteristic microscopic changes in tissues taken from the subcutaneous nodules (mentioned in number 6 above). Again, the province of the pathologist and an area I will always leave to those specialists.

• A diagnosis of *Definite RA* (but not Classic RA) requires only five of those criteria, but again, criteria one through five must be continuous for at least six weeks and there must be none of the exclusions.

• A diagnosis of *Probable RA* requires only three of the above criteria, with at least one of the first five criteria present for at least four weeks. These patients are the ones that a physician might need to follow over a few years to see if other of the criteria finally appear.

• A diagnosis of *Possible RA* requires only two of the following six criteria:

1. Morning stiffness.
2. Physician-observed tenderness or pain with movement of joints recurring over, or lasting through, three weeks.
3. History of *or* physician-observed joint swelling.
4. Physician-observed subcutaneous nodules.
5. Elevated sedimentation rate (the ESR blood test).
6. Iritis (inflammation of the iris of the eye)—this may be of greater value in children with RA.

*The Exclusions.* If any of the following criteria are present, a diagnosis of RA is not made. This list is by no means a comprehensive one, but encompasses the other inherited arthritides we have examined.

1. Evidence of SLE (such as the typical butterfly rash, a high number of LE cells, or a positive ANA test) determined by blood test or clinical examination by a physician.

2. Evidence of gouty arthritis, such as relapsing attacks of redness, swelling, and pain in one or more joints, associated with crystals of uric acid in the joints, or gouty tophi (these are lumpy deposits of the uric acid in the soft tissues).

3. Signs and symptoms suggesting an acute infectious (or septic) arthritis occurring when a person is ill with a known infectious viral or bacterial disease with fever and chills. If the laboratory can grow the infecting agent from the joint fluid, the septic diagnosis is made, but such is not always the case. (Some bacteria and most viruses are quite finicky about being grown under artificial conditions in the laboratory.)

4. A clinical picture that suggests Reiter's syndrome—i.e., arthritis associated with urinary tract and eye symptoms, the urethritis and conjunctivitis we covered in chapter 3.

5. Presence of another major systemic disease that could confuse the picture. Here, I will lump many other medical categories together under one banner. Exclude RA in the presence of any of the following disorders: weakness of the muscles of the neck, trunk, and throat; persistent muscle swelling; the disease dermatomyositis, an inflammatory disease involving skin and muscles that is proven by biopsy and microscopic examination of the tissues; definite scleroderma, a disease that causes fibrous "hardening" of the skin; finding the bacterium that causes tuberculosis in the joint tissues; a strange syndrome called "shoulder/hand," which affects only these two parts of the body with first swelling and then, finally, with muscle wasting; bone changes suggesting the presence of undetected lung cancer or severe lung disease; destructive joint changes typical of a long-standing syphilis infection; blood diseases such as leukemia, lymphoma, or multiple myeloma.

## Criteria of Systemic Lupus Erythematosus (SLE)

To make the diagnosis of SLE, any four of the following eleven criteria must be present at some time during the course

of the disease. They may occur one after another or simultaneously.

1. Butterfly (or so-called malar) rash on the face.
2. Discoid rash: reddened, scaly patches on the skin that
   may form white flat (atrophic) scars over time.
3. Photosensitivity: a skin rash develops with exposure to
   sunlight. The rash is usually a slightly red, slightly bumpy,
   measlelike rash. (Many drugs can cause this kind of reaction, too.)
4. Physician-observed ulcers in the mouth or throat that are
   painless.
5. Arthritis: tenderness, swelling, or fluid involving two or
   more peripheral joints, with an arthritis that does not
   erode the bones.
6. Serositis: painful inflammation and often fluid accumu-
   lation in the lining over the lungs (pleurisy and pleural
   effusion) or the heart (pericarditis and pericardial effusion). The inflamed tissues create friction when they move
   across one another, which can cause a rubbing sound (a
   "rub") that a physician can hear through a stethoscope.
   To qualify on this count, either the physician must hear
   the rub or verify the presence of the fluid.
7. Kidney disorders: spilling protein into the urine or the
   presence of "casts," which give evidence of inflammation
   and damage in the kidney. These casts are nothing more
   than deposits of debris from red or white blood cells into
   the tiny tubes of the kidney. This debris is flushed out
   into the urine.
8. Nervous system disorders such as seizures or psychoses
   (severe mental or emotional imbalances) that cannot be
   explained by reactions to medications or other illnesses.
9. Blood disorders such as anemia caused by destruction of
   red blood cells, low counts of white blood cells or platelets
   (cells that help clot the blood).
10. Immune system changes: the tests we spoke of earlier,

including positive LE prep, or other tests for such nuclear antibodies. An interesting finding is that some people with SLE will show a *false* positive result for the screening test for syphilis. By that I mean they don't actually have syphilis, although the screening test is positive. Further tests for that disease will always be negative.

11. A high level of antinuclear antibodies (ANA) when none of the lupus-causing medications mentioned in chapter 3 could be responsible.


**Criteria for Acute Gouty Arthritis**

The signs and symptoms in A, B, and C confirm the diagnosis of gout.

A. Uric acid (urate) crystals in fluid from an arthritic joint.

B. A gouty tophus, a skin nodule or lump that contains the urate crystals. (Note: Many of my patients who I know currently have gouty arthritis do not have tophi. These take time to develop, and in fact may never do so in some people.)

C. The presence of any six of these twelve criteria:

1. More than one attack of acute arthritis with redness, swelling, and pain in the same joint.
2. Rapid onset of joint symptoms—development of the maximum amount of pain and inflammation in a single day.
3. Arthritic attack of a single joint never progressing to involve any others (monoarticular arthritis).
4. Physician-observed joint redness.
5. Painful swelling of the metatarsal-phalangeal (MTP) joint (where the toe joins the foot) of the great toe.
6. Attack of that first MTP joint in only one foot.
7. Arthritic attack in the tarsal joint (where the foot joins onto the ankle) of only one foot.
8. A skin nodule presumed to be a tophus (but unavailable for sampling).
9. Elevated blood uric acid.

10. X-ray evidence of swelling within a joint appreciably more in one of a pair of joints than the other.
11. X-ray evidence of cysts in the bone beneath the outer layer of bony cortex without the "erosions" of RA.
12. Negative cultures. This means the joint fluid withdrawn during an attack fails to "grow" any infecting germ in the laboratory.


### The Spondylopathies

Although we have no formal set of diagnostic criteria for these diseases as we do for RA, SLE, and gout, they each have important diagnostic features that I will discuss briefly here.

*Ankylosing Spondylitis.* The single *sine qua non*—the sign on which a diagnosis rests and without which it cannot be made—for AS is X-ray evidence of inflammation in the sacroiliac (SI) joints of the lower back. Unless this finding is present in a case of spinal arthritis, you can't call it AS. It may be one of the other arthritides that involve the back, such as psoriasis, ulcerative colitis, or Crohn's disease, but it's not AS. And, although the inflammation will proceed to involve more of the spine ultimately, the arthritic changes will always first be visible in the SI joints.

In all cases of spinal arthritis—even with X-ray proof of inflammation of the SI joints—the physician must search for clues that would implicate one of the other causes of back inflammation before diagnosing AS. The first step of the search would be to probe for a history of skin or bowel problems. If such a history turns up, then the physician would try to verify those clues by various means. Let's look at a few.

*Punch Biopsy of the Skin.* For example, if the patient has skin plaques typical of psoriasis, then that might lead to taking a biopsy (removal of a very small sample of the inflamed skin) for the pathologist to examine under the microscope. Changes characteristic of psoriasis would clinch the diagnosis of psoriatic arthritis of the spine.

Taking the sample of skin involves first numbing the area with an anesthetic agent, then gently removing a circular piece of skin, using a "punch" biopsy tool. The tool works much like a tiny cookie cutter, removes a core of skin, and leaves a small punched-out hole that heals easily.

*Intestinal X-Ray Studies, Colonoscopy, and Bowel Biopsy.* If, however, the patient suffered relapsing bouts of diarrhea, abdominal cramping, and bloating, the next diagnostic step might be to get either special X-ray studies of the intestine— called an upper GI (gastrointestinal) series and a barium enema—or perhaps a trip to the gastroenterologist (the bowel specialist) for direct examination of the colon.

In the X-ray examinations of the upper portion of the bowel, the patient must drink a "barium malt," which tastes something like strawberry chalk. Once that's down, the patient lies on an examination table, which the radiologist tilts at various angles. X-ray pictures are taken as the barium solution traverses the upper bowel. The barium in the solution shows up bright white on the X rays, and because the solution fills up the intestine as it moves along, it outlines the shape of the inside of it for us to see in the picture. (I have done this one myself, and although it's not something I would seek out to do for fun, it really wasn't all that bad.)

The X-ray examination of the lower part of the intestine, however, requires a different approach. The only feasible way to fill the colon with a barium solution is to use an enema. (Although I have not had to undergo this test personally, from all reports it's somewhat uncomfortable, as you might imagine.) Once the fluid is in place, the X-ray pictures begin. And once again, the barium clings to the walls of the bowel, outlining its shape, size, and any abnormalities that might be there.

Ultimately, however, because the diagnosis of either of these inflammatory conditions of the gut will rest on a biopsy of the bowel, most patients will come to colonoscopy. In this kind of study, the examining physician (usually a specialist in intestinal diseases) actually looks up into the bowel with a flexible fiber-optic light. Through the magic of such technology, the physician can see the inside of the bowel as the scope passes along (in some ways analogous to the way a periscope on a submarine lets the captain see the surface above). Also, the physician can insert, through the slender flexible length of the scope, a tiny biopsy forcep (like a little pruning tool) to take a tissue sample for the pathologist to examine under the microscope. The information gained on biopsy of these tissues forms the basis for the diagnosis of ulcerative colitis or Crohn's disease.

For those of you who have family members undergoing these and other tests, I hope that knowing a little more about them has helped to demystify them. And for those readers still searching to put the pieces together of your family's arthritic history, I hope that this presentation of the medical criteria in layman's terms has made your investigation easier. With this information and the help of your family physician, you should be able to make more educated guesses to fill in some of the diagnostic holes in your family genogram.

# 7

# Current Treatment Methods and Prevention of Crippling Through Early Treatment

You and I have a common bond. We are not arthritic, but we have a family history that increases our risk of becoming so. And although I hope that you intend to join me in living a life-style that helps to reduce the risk, we must recognize that the possibility of arthritic development—our genetic message—remains. Many of us have watched relatives who have suffered the pain and crippling of arthritis. And we don't want that fate to befall us or our children. But what does traditional medicine have to offer us if it should?

For many years, physicians had little to offer those afflicted with arthritis beyond the therapeutic advantages of a hot bath and some medicines to relieve the pain a little. It wasn't until the 1960s and 1970s that specific medicines to combat the inflammatory process arrived and physicians first used some of the potent "disease-modifying" drugs, such as the antimalarials. (These drugs, still in use for both purposes, were first used to combat malaria, and the name persists.) Thankfully, these treatment methods did help some patients, but in others, the crippling continued.

In the last decade or two, some very powerful drugs (ones used to combat cancers and the like) and artificial joint replacement surgeries also appeared on the scene, but for the most part we did not pull them out of our black bags until the arthritic inflammation and crippling had become severe and would not respond to lesser therapies. Reluctance to use these powerful drugs stemmed primarily from the fact that the treatments themselves were not without risk of serious side effects.

However, in recent years, the complexion of arthritis treatment has begun to change. More and more, arthritis specialists have begun to intervene early in the course of such diseases as RA, trying to stop the process *before* it leads to crippling. Their greater willingness to begin these potent therapies sooner has come about in part because continued research—much of it thanks to the generosity of supporters of the Arthritis Foundation—has refined these drug and surgical therapies and made them much safer. (Remember our guiding precept: First do no harm. With each and every therapy, a physician must weigh the potential for good against the potential for harm. And the scale has to tip to the good side or you're better off without that treatment.)

Turn with me now for a look at the basic methods of treatment for arthritic diseases. I don't intend to dwell on them at great length—there are entire books devoted to such subjects—however I do think it's important to at least acquaint you with them, especially because many of you may presently or eventually have family members who need to undergo such treatment. Some of the potential side effects of the drugs used to treat arthritis may sound frightening to you, and although these things *can* and *do* happen, the vast majority of patients who take these medications do so unscathed. I do not intend this information to alarm any of you who have relatives taking one or more of these drugs, or to frighten you into taking care to prevent arthritis—although certainly anything I do to increase preventive measures cannot be a bad thing. That said, let's proceed.

# Drug Therapy

## NSAID

NSAID stands for nonsteroid anti-inflammatory drug, short-ened for obvious reasons. This class of drugs, of which plain old honest aspirin is the prototype, suppress or reduce the degree of inflammation in arthritic joints. They do so by inhibiting the body's production of inflammatory prostaglandins and other chemical messengers of inflammation, but they do not have any effect on the underlying disease process. They exert their effect while you take them, and the effect quickly wanes when you stop them.

NSAIDs are not without potentially serious side effects, how-ever. The most common of these are irritation to the stomach lining even to the point of actual bleeding ulcers, diarrhea or cramping, blood thinning and bleeding problems, liver damage of a temporary nature (it usually disappears as soon as the patient stops the drug), ringing in the ears, allergic reactions ranging from rash to life-threatening anaphylaxis, increase in intestinal permeability (which could worsen food allergies or intolerances), and kidney impairment.

The currently used drugs of the NSAID class with brand names in parentheses are aspirin and other salycilates (Ecotrin, Easprin, Trilisate, Salflex), ibuprofen (Motrin, Rufen), phenylbutazone (Butazoladin), indomethacin (Indocin), sulindac (Clinoril), na-proxen (Naprosyn, Anaprox), tolmetin (Tolectin), fenoprofen (Nalfon), meclofenamate sodium (Meclomen), diflunisal (Do-lobid), piroxicam (Feldene), ketoprofen (Orudis), and the newest entrant to the field, etodolac (Lodine).

## Disease-Modifying Drugs

This diverse assortment of drugs have the common end result of slowing or halting the actual progression of the arthritic dis-ease. They do not offer immediate advantages—like the NSAIDs do—of pain and inflammation relief, but rather exert their effects slowly over time. Gradually, the signs and symptoms of arthritis disappear in those patients who respond to therapy, and the remissions may be total or last for prolonged periods.

Some of these drugs appear to work by suppressing the overactive immune system response, whereas others in the class act by unknown means. The original development for most of them was to treat diseases other than arthritis; their usefulness for arthritic improvement was discovered after the fact. And although I have said that there is a move toward using these drugs earlier in the course of rheumatic diseases, and that they are considered safe, they are not a panacea. Not every arthritic patient will benefit, and some patients may experience severe reactions to the drugs. Remember, these are all potent medications that should only be administered by a physician skilled in their use and ready to respond to their possible adverse effects.

*The Antimalarials.*   These drugs—chloroquine and hydroxy-chloroquine—designed to ward off malaria or treat patients who develop it—also happen to slowly suppress the symptoms of such inherited arthritic diseases as SLE and RA. Although researchers know quite a lot about the effect of these drugs on various parts of the immune system, exactly what action accounts for arthritic response remains a mystery.

The toxic effects of these drugs range from serious damage to the retina of the eye to dermatitis (a skin inflammation causing a rash or peeling) to nausea and diarrhea to anemia. My father suffered a severe form of dermatitis when he took a drug from this group.

*Gold Compounds.*   The first use of gold salts to treat arthritis dates back to the 1920s, with renewed interest in their use occurring in the 1960s. Recently an oral or pill form of gold has become available, but prior to that development, the only means of giving gold was in shot form (which is still done). The normal course spaces the injections a week apart until the patient responds with maximum benefit. Then, normally, the patients shift to a maintenance dose about once a month as long as they tolerate the medication and continue to respond favorably.

Gold was the mainstay of my father's therapy. He held the

dubious distinction of having received more gold salts than any living human—having received weekly maximum dose shots for about fifteen years, although his disease still raged. It didn't seem to me at the time that his therapy did much good; as I told you before, his sedimentation rates even on therapy ran very high. And when I was a teenager, I recall saying to him, "Daddy, if those shots aren't helping, why do you keep on getting them every week?" And he responded, "Sugar, maybe they are. And if this is what it's like with them, I don't want to know what it would be like without them." He understood the basic truth about disease-modifying therapy: It may not seem to be working because the relief of symptoms is so gradual.

Although research has shown that gold compounds do reduce inflammation, suppress the activity of various immune cells, and slow the erosive damage to the joints, precisely how they achieve these results is still unknown.

Toxic side effects include itching and rashing of the skin (in as many as one out of four patients), kidney damage, mouth ulcers, and blood disorders. The oral form of the drug has seemed to cause fewer of these side effects than the injectable form.

*Penicillamine.* This drug, a distant relative of penicillin, binds to heavy metals in the body. Its main use prior to the 1960s, when it first began to be used in arthritis, was to chelate (surround and remove) such heavy metals as copper, lead, and mercury in cases of poisoning. Once again, its precise mode of action in reducing inflammation in arthritis is unknown; however, complete remission of symptoms may occur in some patients placed on this therapy. (It was, in fact, on penicillamine therapy that my father's sedimentation rate fell to reasonable levels for the first time in fifteen or so years of disease. Whether this drug caused the improvement or the disease had just begun to burn out on its own, we'll never know.)

Although the drug can be quite effective, as many as one-third of patients do not tolerate taking it. Common side effects include dermatitis, loss of appetite and weight loss, nausea, vomiting, diarrhea, and less often, kidney damage.

*Sulfasalazine.*   A derivative of the aspirin and sulfa antibiotic families, this drug appears to benefit both RA patients and those with ulcerative colitis. It may also prove useful in Reiter's syndrome and AS. Because of its sulfa base, those patients with a history of sulfa drug allergies cannot take it.

The spectrum of toxic side effects is much less for this disease modifier than for some of the others. As many as 20 percent of patients stop the drug because of intestinal intolerance (nausea, vomiting, and diarrhea) and as many as 5 percent more for rashes.

*Methotrexate.* This drug—which is a chemical similar to the vitamin folic acid, but about 1 million times more potent—is used regularly in cancer chemotherapy. Although it strongly suppresses the immune system, its chief role in rheumatoid arthritic therapy is to slow down the growth of the actively dividing, inflamed, angry synovial (joint-lining) tissues; thereby preventing those exuberant tissues from eroding and destroying the joint.

A relatively newly approved, once-a-week oral form of the drug for use in RA (Rheumatrex) is now available.

Severe toxic side effects include suppression of the bone marrow (where blood cells and infection-fighting cells are made); severe mouth ulcers; damage to the intestinal lining, causing diarrhea, nausea, and vomiting; hair loss; and liver damage.

### Corticosteroids

Our bodies naturally produce steroid compounds in response to stress, infection, and inflammation, but sometimes in amounts inadequate to the task. To fill that gap, modern pharmacy has provided us a wide variety of synthetic ones in shot form, as pills, or as lotions, ointments, or drops applied to the skin or eyes. They lack the fine control of our natural steroids. But they do have a place in the treatment of inflammatory diseases, if used judiciously.

Corticosteroids potently inhibit inflammation and suppress the overactive immune response in the inherited arthritides (and many, many other conditions as well). In fact, patients with severely inflamed arthritic joints can reap almost instant improvement of symptoms from a healthy dose of steroid; they hurt much less, can move more freely, and experience an improved sense of well-being. The relief is so dramatic, that it's almost magic. And therein lies the danger of steroids.

No physician likes to see a patient in pain. After all, relieving pain and suffering where possible is one of the goals of medicine. And for the arthritic patient, steroid doses do that very thing. The problem is, that's not all they do. And here, once again, we run head on into that guiding precept of medical care: First do no harm. Too frequent administration of steroid drugs overrides our bodies' built-in regulation system. The regulation of natural release of our steroids from our adrenal glands depends on the level of steroid hormones in our blood. When those levels stay artificially high (from doses of synthetic steroid) for too long a time, our glands will no longer respond to a need to release steroid. Because the steroid molecules have a whole host of other important functions besides relieving inflammation, we must have them to survive. If we can no longer make and release them naturally, we become dependent on taking the drug in pill or shot form.

The danger of steroid use lies in the fact that the severe side effects take time to develop. The instant gratification of pain and symptom relief is all that a patient can see at the time. It is difficult for patients to understand why they can't have more of this wonder drug that makes them feel so great. The specter of steroid dependency hides in the shadowy future. It's the physician's job to reserve the use of steroid for the worst of times, for as short a time as possible, and then to taper the drug slowly to coax the adrenal glands back into action.

My father's arthritic inflammation was so extreme that his physician did have to resort to the use of steroids to just keep some cap on the progress of his disease. And, as a result, he became steroid dependent, with all of its attendant health problems. Among these are damage to the heart muscle (steroid cardiomyopathy), wasting of the skeletal muscles, thinning of the skin, easy bruising, a change in the location of body fat (deposited in the cheeks, the belly, and back of the neck), and weakening of the bones. He took daily steroids (interspersed with shots of ACTH—a hormone—to try to stimulate release of natural steroid from his adrenal glands) until he died.

The moral to that story is that corticosteroids can be a powerful tool in treating arthritis, but like a two-edged sword, they must be treated with respect and handled with caution.

## Joint Replacement

The development of surgical technology in recent decades has made it possible to remove shattered hips, destroyed knees, and immobile wrists and replace them with artifical joints. I have assisted in such operations, and they are indeed magic.

In most cases, the replacement procedures involve removal of joints already severely crippled by arthritis, shattering trauma, or infection. (My father underwent two such operations—a hip and a knee—in his quest to walk freely again. He was quite pleased with the results, not in the least because these two joints were the only two in his body that didn't hurt.)

In recent years, some orthopedic hand surgeons have begun to recommend early replacement of the wrist in patients with rheumatoid arthritis. Severe crippling of the hands in RA can create the most burdensome handicap of all, and preventing it changes the complexion of life for such patients. For most of us, functional fingers and hands are an absolute necessity for daily life. Think about it. What if it were a thirty-minute chore to button your shirt? What if you couldn't do that at all? How about opening a jar of peanut butter? Writing a check? Signing a form? If your hips or knees go, you can survive in a wheelchair. But what do you do for hands?

The classic deformity of the hands in RA comes about by an imbalance in the pull of muscles, tendons, and ligaments across the unstable wrist. Stabilizing the wrist, therefore, is the key to stopping the process. Intervening *before* the deformities begin— when only changes on X ray and subtle muscle function losses foreshadow the coming problems—by replacing the diseased wrist with an artificial model, can prevent most of the crippling hand deformities and preserve function. The development and widespread use of this kind of surgery arrived too late for my father. In his hands, I could read every documented deformity associated with RA. But gnarled and profoundly crippled as they were, he continued to use them to pursue his photography hobby, to peck at the keys of his electric typewriter, to putter from his wheelchair about the house and all over town.

The key is prevention. And I urge any of you with arthritic relatives to contact your local Arthritis Foundation office or the chapter office nearest you. Find out what kinds of physical therapy, surgical therapy, medical therapy, and exercise therapy might be available that you are unaware of. Take advantage of whatever current medicine has to offer to keep the arthritic patient functioning at top capacity.

# 8

# In Search of the Golden Mean

The Greeks had their own concept of perfection: the golden mean. They understood that the quality of life rested in maintaining the proper balance of all its elements. In other words, take all things in moderation, nothing to excess.

In our quest to prevent the expression of our genetic message, to preserve and protect our health, you and I must adhere to that principle. Although we must not neglect our physical well-being, it is just as important not to neglect our emotional, mental, and spiritual health. Our goal must be to find that golden mean, to achieve a harmonious balance among all the elements in our lives, taking time to attend to the ongoing maintenance of each of them. Because if we neglect even one of these aspects, the others suffer and falter.

So far, we've examined the benefits of proper nutrition and the dangers of the lack of it. We've looked at the importance of regular conditioning exercise. Now let's turn to the other component of complete health: maintaining spiritual or emotional health, and the corollary of effectively living and coping with the stresses of adult life.

Recall that I mentioned early in the book, that my father laid the development of his arthritic disease at the door of exhaustion from extreme physical and emotional stress. Could that be so? Is there any medical validity to an old wives' tale that would have us believe that living under stress can ruin your health? Yes. From my own clinical practice, I can tell you that this folk belief is absolutely correct.

I see it almost daily in my general practice, the woman packing and moving to a new home coming down with a bladder infection, men in the throes of divorce developing stomach ulcers, brides on the eve of their weddings falling victim to strep throat, businesspeople returning from Tokyo developing chest colds. And the lament is always the same: "I don't have time for this." I commiserate with them, I understand, and I tell them that during such times—when you're so overburdened with work or plans that you can't take time out to rest and recuperate—is precisely when you will get sick. And there's a real medical reason for it.

In recent years, modern medical technology has enabled us to accurately measure various components of our immune system and to assess how well they function. What research has discovered is that at times of physical or emotional stress, circulating levels of antibodies (remember those infection-fighting products of our immune cells) fall dramatically. Their decline leaves a window of opportunity for any potential invader from the germ world that happens to be in the vicinity.

In medicine, we speak of the Theory of Fertile Ground in relation to infections and cancers. Day in and day out, we humans are assailed by viruses, bacteria, fungi, and cells from our own bodies "gone bad." As I mentioned in chapter 3, we depend on our healthy, normally functioning immune system to defend us against this onslaught. However, if we suffer a dip in our resistance, a decline in our immunity—whether from exhaustion, aging, poor nutrition, or stress—these invaders may more easily take root. In effect, we become more "fertile ground" in which the seeds of infection or cancer can flower.

We can't change the fact that life in the real world will be fraught with real-world stresses. In fact, the field of psychiatry has even cataloged the major stresses of adult life and ranked them in order of how stressful they are. Among the most oppressing of the major stresses are death of a parent, spouse, or child; serious illness of a parent, spouse, or child; serious personal illness; divorce; loss of a job; changing jobs; changing homes. Unfortunately, most of us will have to suffer several of these in the course of our lives. And sometimes, we must deal with more than one of them at once. What makes the difference to us in how we handle those stresses is the condition (physical and emotional) that we're in when we must meet them. Maintaining ourselves in that physically strong, emotionally sound shape takes daily effort, and it requires us to search for the golden mean in our lives.

My husband and I recently ran across a book—which has been a best-seller for some time—that helped us to find and keep the balance in our lives. I recommend it to you as an invaluable tool in your quest for harmony. The book is *The Seven Habits of Highly Effective People* by Stephen R. Covey. This book causes you to rethink your priorities, to make time for those things that are truly important to you in the long haul—not those seemingly important at the moment. Week by week, it requires you assess the roles you must play in life (for me, mother, spouse, doctor, writer, individual) and to write down the goals you want to achieve in each of those roles. Then, you must schedule your week's efforts to fulfill your goals in all areas: making time for physical conditioning, mental improvement, social and emotional concerns, and spiritual exercise. The best feature of this kind of planning, however, is that you can look at this schedule and immediately recognize that you have devoted too much time to one facet of your life and neglected or overlooked others.

If you can keep all aspects of your life in balance, if you can make the time to build and nurture healthy, close, relationships with family and friends, if you can strive to improve mental sharpness and physical health, you will be in better condition to handle whatever curve life may throw you. And like my father, you will be able to approach any adversity with the phrase I heard him use a million times: "That ain't no hill for a stepper."

# 9

# Resources

In this chapter, I have compiled a listing of all the sources and resources I have mentioned in the book. I hope that you will find them helpful.

## Arthritis Foundation

For information about arthritis, ranging from current therapies to assistance for patients with arthritis, to exercise programs, to the newest in research, write to:

> Arthritis Foundation
> P.O. Box 19000
> Atlanta, GA 30326

Or call the local chapter nearest you.

**Alabama Chapter**
Birmingham, AL
(205) 870–4700

**South Alabama Chapter**
Mobile, AL
(205) 432–7171

**Alaska Unit**
Anchorage, AK
(907) 274–2373

**Central Arizona Chapter**
Phoenix, AZ
(602) 264–7679

**Southern Arizona Chapter**
Tucson, AZ
(602) 326–2811

**Arkansas Chapter**
Little Rock, AR
(501) 664–7242

**Northeastern California Chapter**
Sacramento, CA
(916) 921–5533

**Northern California Chapter**
San Francisco, CA
(415) 673–6882

**San Diego Area Chapter**
San Diego, CA
(619) 492–1094

**Southern California Chapter**
Los Angeles, CA
(213) 938–6111

**Rocky Mountain Chapter**
Denver, CO
(303) 756–8622

**Connecticut Chapter**
Rocky Hill, CT
(203) 563–1177

**Delaware Chapter**
Wilmington, DE
(302) 764–8254

**Metropolitan Washington Chapter**
Arlington, VA
(703) 276–7555

**Florida Chapter**
Bradenton, FL
(813) 795–3010

**Georgia Chapter**
Atlanta, GA
(404) 351–0454

**Hawaii Chapter**
Honolulu, HI
(808) 523–7561

**Idaho Chapter**
Boise, ID
(208) 344–7102

**Illinois Chapter**
Chicago, IL
(312) 782–1367

**Central Illinois Chapter**
Peoria, IL
(309) 682–6337

**Indiana Chapter**
Indianapolis, IN
(317) 879–0321

**Iowa Chapter**
Des Moines, IA
(515) 278–0636

**Kansas Chapter**
Wichita, KS
(316) 263–0116

**Kentucky Chapter**
Louisville, KY
(502) 893–9771

**Louisiana Chapter**
New Orleans, LA
(504) 387–6932

**Maine Chapter**
Brunswick, ME
(207) 729–4453

**Maryland Chapter**
Lutherville, MD
(301) 561–8090

**Massachusetts Chapter**
Newton, MA
(617) 244–1800

**Michigan Chapter**
Southfield, MI
(313) 350–3030

**Minnesota Chapter**
Minneapolis, MN
(612) 874–1201

**Mississippi Chapter**
Jackson, MS
(601) 956–3371

**Eastern Missouri Chapter**
St. Louis, MO
(314) 644–3488

**Western Missouri—Greater Kansas City Chapter**
Kansas City, MO
(816) 361–7002

**Montana Chapter**
Billings, MT
(406) 248–7602

**Nebraska Chapter**
Omaha, NE
(402) 391–8000

**Nevada Chapter**
Las Vegas, NV
(702) 367–1626

**New Hampshire Chapter**
Concord, NH
(603) 244–9322

**New Jersey Chapter**
Iselin, NJ
(201) 283–4300

**New Mexico Chapter**
Albuquerque, NM
(505) 265–1545

**Central New York Chapter**
Syracuse, NY
(315) 455–8553

**Genesee Valley Chapter**
Rochester, NY
(716) 423–9490

**Long Island Chapter**
Melville, NY
(516) 427–8272

**New York Chapter**
New York, NY
(212) 477–8310

**Northeastern New York Chapter**
Albany, NY
(518) 459–5082

**Western New York Chapter**
Tonawanda, NY
(716) 837–8600

**North Carolina Chapter**
Durham, NC
(919) 596–3360

**Dakota Chapter**
Fargo, ND
(701) 237–3310

**Central Ohio Chapter**
Columbus, OH
(614) 488–0777

**Northeastern Ohio Chapter**
Cleveland, OH
(216) 791–1310

**Northwestern Ohio Chapter**
Toledo, OH
(419) 537–0888

**Southwestern Ohio Chapter**
Cincinnati, OH
(513) 271–4545

**Eastern Oklahoma Chapter**
Tulsa, OK
(918) 743–4526

**Oklahoma Chapter**
Oklahoma City, OK
(405) 521–0066

**Oregon Chapter**
Portland, OR
(503) 222–7246

**Central Pennsylvania Chapter**
Camp Hill, PA
(717) 763–0900

**Eastern Pennsylvania Chapter**
Philadelphia, PA
(215) 574–9480

**Western Pennsylvania Chapter**
Pittsburgh, PA
(412) 566–1645

**Rhode Island Chapter**
East Providence, RI
(401) 434–5792

**South Carolina Chapter**
Columbia, SC
(803) 254–6702

**Middle-East Tennessee Chapter**
Nashville, TN
(615) 329–3431

**West Tennessee Chapter**
Memphis, TN
(901) 365–7080

**North Texas Chapter**
Dallas, TX
(214) 826–4361

**Northwest Texas Chapter**
Fort Worth, TX
(817) 926–7733

**South Central Texas Chapter**
San Antonio, TX
(512) 224–8222

**Texas Gulf Coast Chapter**
Houston, TX
(713) 785–2360

**Utah Chapter**
Salt Lake City, UT
(801) 486–4993

**Vermont & Northern
New York Chapter**
Burlington, VT
(802) 864–4988

**Virginia Chapter**
Richmond, VA
(804) 270–1229

**Washington State Chapter**
Seattle, WA
(206) 622–1378

**Wisconsin Chapter**
West Allis, WI
(414) 321–3933

For Canadian arthritis societies, write to:

**The Arthritis Society National Office**
250 Bloor Street E., Suite 401
Toronto, Ontario
M4W 3P2
Canada

**The Arthritis Society
Newfoundland Division**
P.O. Box 522, Station C
St. John's, Newfoundland
A1C 5K4
Canada

**The Arthritis Society
Prince Edward Island Division**
P.O. Box 1537
Charlottetown, Prince Edward Island
C1A 7N3
Canada

**The Arthritis Society
Nova Scotia Division**
5516 Spring Garden Road
Halifax, Nova Scotia
B3J 1G6
Canada

**The Arthritis Society
Ontario Division**
250 Bloor Street E., Suite 401
Toronto, Ontario
M4W 3P2
Canada

**The Arthritis Society
Manitoba Division**
386 Broadway Avenue, Suite 105
Winnipeg, Manitoba
R3C 3R6
Canada

**The Arthritis Society
Saskatchewan Division**
2078 Halifax Street
Regina, Saskatchewan
S4P 1T7
Canada

**The Arthritis Society
Alberta Division**
301, 1301-8th Street S.W.
Calgary, Alberta
T2R 1B7
Canada

The Arthritis Society
New Brunswick Division
65 Brunswick Street
Fredericton, New Brunswick
E3B 1G5
Canada

The Arthritis Society British Columbia and Yukon Division
895 West 10th Avenue
Vancouver, British Columbia
V5Z 1L7
Canada

The Arthritis Society
Quebec Division
2075 University Street, Suite 1206
Montreal, Quebec
H3A 2L1
Canada

## Arthritis Foundation Publications

The following is a listing of most of the publications from the Arthritis Foundation. These either are free or are available for a nominal charge.

*Arthritis Medical Information Series.* Pamphlets written in layman's terms covering a number of arthritic conditions, including arthritis in children, arthritis and inflammatory bowel disease, ankylosing spondylitis, back pain, gout, psoriatic arthritis, Reiter's syndrome, rheumatoid arthritis, lupus, and a host of other, less common, muscle, bone, and joint disorders.

*Medication Briefs.* Question-and-answer pamphlets about side effects, dosages, and recommendations for taking such medications as gold salts, hydroxychloroquine, methotrexate, azathioprine, penicillamine, cyclophosphamide, phenylbutazone, and a general guide to medications.

Also available are pamphlets titled: *The Family: Making the Difference; Guide to Insurance for People with Arthritis; Help Your Doctor—Help Yourself to a Better Partnership; Living and Loving: Information about Sex; Practical Information: Where to Turn for Help; When Your Student Has Arthritis: A Guide for Teachers; Surgery: Information to Consider; Taking Care: Protecting Your Joints and Saving Your Energy; Taking Charge: Learning to Live with Arthritis; Unproven Remedies; Arthritis Materials for Health Professionals; Arthritis Research: What's New.*

*Arthritis Today* is a magazine, published every two months, that gives information, advice, and research updates. A minimum contribution of $15 to the Arthritis Foundation entitles you to receive a subscription.

For those readers interested in a much more in-depth and scientific presentation of the arthritides, you can purchase (through the Arthritis Foundation) a copy of *Primer on Rheumatic Diseases*, now in its ninth edition. This soft-cover book is highly technical, for the most part, and designed for physicians in training or practice. But anyone with a fairly strong background in the life sciences and biochemistry would find it interesting and understandable.

In its classes, the Arthritis Foundation recommends the good self-management resource book *The Arthritis Helpbook* written by Kate Lorig and James F. Fries (see Bibliography). It delves into diet, exercises, pain management, medications, and sleeping problems and gives hints to make dressing, housework, driving, and bathing easier for the arthritic person.

## Fatty Acid Supplements—Mail-Order Source

Omega-3 and Omega-6 Fatty Acid Supplements
BioSyn
21 Tioga Way
Marblehead, MA 01945
Telephone: (800) 346–2703

## Stop-Smoking Regimens

A number of effective programs in community hospitals, medical centers, and private clinics to treat smoking addiction have opened in recent years, using every method of treatment from behavior modification to aversion therapy to hypnosis.

In the stop-smoking program we run through our practice,

we have used several methods that seem to work. Let your doctor decide if any of the following treatments might work for you.

1. Catapress patches seem to reduce the nicotine craving. These patches are prescribed in the same dose a doctor would use to treat for hypertension. We have found that smokers generally must use the patches for three or four weeks while they try to quit.

2. Doxepin (Adapin) at bedtime. We start with a dose of 25 to 50 milligrams per day and slowly increase the dose to 100 or 150 milligrams over a few weeks. Once at the upper-limit dose, the patient makes the commitment to stop smoking; he or she should find the expected anxiety and withdrawal much less uncomfortable. We continue to prescribe the doxepin for several weeks after the patient has stopped smoking, and then we slowly taper the dose and discontinue the drug.

3. Spheopalatine ganglion block is a technique that uses 1 percent lidocaine (or better, 0.75 percent marcaine) applied topically through the nose to numb the ganglion and prevent withdrawal from nicotine. Once the patient has made the commitment to quit smoking, he or she must undergo the block for twenty minutes duration on five consecutive days. The patient must not smoke or chew nicotine gum, because that defeats the purpose of the procedure, which is to block the withdrawal symptoms. We use this as only part of a full program that combines group counseling, Catapress patches, and a mild anxiolytic (anxiety-reducing drug). If you or your doctor would like more information about our program, please write to our clinic:

> Medi-Stat Medical Clinic
> 8116 Cantrell Road
> Little Rock, AR 72207

Food and Nutrition Board, National Academy of Sciences—National Research Council Recommended Dietary Allowances[a]

| Category | Age (years) or Condition | Weight[b] (kg) | (lb) | Height[b] (cm) | (in) | Protein (g) | Fat-Soluble Vitamins Vitamin A (mg RE)[c] | Vitamin D (mg)[d] | Vitamin E (mg a-TE)[e] | Vitamin K (mg) |
|---|---|---|---|---|---|---|---|---|---|---|
| Infants | 0.0–0.5 | 6 | 13 | 60 | 24 | 13 | 375 | 7.5 | 3 | 5 |
|  | 0.5–1.0 | 9 | 20 | 71 | 28 | 14 | 375 | 10 | 4 | 10 |
| Children | 1–3 | 13 | 29 | 90 | 35 | 16 | 400 | 10 | 6 | 15 |
|  | 4–6 | 20 | 44 | 112 | 44 | 24 | 500 | 10 | 7 | 20 |
|  | 7–10 | 28 | 62 | 132 | 52 | 28 | 700 | 10 | 7 | 30 |
| Males | 11–14 | 45 | 99 | 157 | 62 | 45 | 1,000 | 10 | 10 | 45 |
|  | 15–18 | 66 | 145 | 176 | 69 | 59 | 1,000 | 10 | 10 | 65 |
|  | 19–24 | 72 | 160 | 177 | 70 | 58 | 1,000 | 10 | 10 | 70 |
|  | 25–50 | 79 | 174 | 176 | 70 | 63 | 1,000 | 5 | 10 | 80 |
|  | 51+ | 77 | 170 | 173 | 68 | 63 | 1,000 | 5 | 10 | 80 |
| Females | 11–14 | 46 | 101 | 157 | 62 | 46 | 800 | 10 | 8 | 45 |
|  | 15–18 | 55 | 120 | 163 | 64 | 44 | 800 | 10 | 8 | 55 |
|  | 19–24 | 58 | 128 | 164 | 65 | 46 | 800 | 10 | 8 | 60 |
|  | 25–50 | 63 | 138 | 163 | 64 | 50 | 800 | 5 | 8 | 65 |
|  | 51+ | 65 | 143 | 160 | 63 | 50 | 800 | 5 | 8 | 65 |
| Pregnant |  |  |  |  |  | 60 | 800 | 10 | 10 | 65 |
| Lactating | 1st 6 months |  |  |  |  | 65 | 1,300 | 10 | 12 | 65 |
|  | 2nd 6 months |  |  |  |  | 62 | 1,200 | 10 | 11 | 65 |

[a]The allowances, expressed as average daily intakes over time, are intended to provide for individual variations among most normal persons as they live in the United States under usual environmental stresses. Diets should be based on a variety of common foods in order to provide other nutrients for which human requirements have been less well defined. This table was revised in 1989.

[b]Weights and heights of reference adults are actual medians for the U.S. population of the designated age, as reported by NHANES II. The median weights and heights of those under 19 years of age were taken from the *American Journal of Clinical Nutrition*, 32:602–629, Hamill et al. (1979). The use of these figures does not imply that the height-to-weight ratios are ideal.

| Category | Water-Soluble Vitamins | | | | | | | Minerals | | | | | | |
|---|---|---|---|---|---|---|---|---|---|---|---|---|---|---|
| | Vitamin C (mg) | Thiamin (mg) | Riboflavin (mg) | Niacin (mg NE)[f] | Vitamin B6 (mg) | Folate (mg) | Vitamin B12 (mg) | Calcium (mg) | Phosphorus (mg) | Magnesium (mg) | Iron (mg) | Zinc (mg) | Iodine (mg) | Selenium (mg) |
| Infants | 30 | 0.3 | 0.4 | 5 | 0.3 | 25 | 0.3 | 400 | 300 | 40 | 6 | 5 | 40 | 10 |
| | 35 | 0.4 | 0.5 | 6 | 0.6 | 35 | 0.5 | 600 | 500 | 60 | 10 | 5 | 50 | 15 |
| Children | 40 | 0.7 | 0.8 | 9 | 1.0 | 50 | 0.7 | 800 | 800 | 80 | 10 | 10 | 70 | 20 |
| | 45 | 0.9 | 1.1 | 12 | 1.1 | 75 | 1.0 | 800 | 800 | 120 | 10 | 10 | 90 | 20 |
| | 45 | 1.0 | 1.2 | 13 | 1.4 | 100 | 1.4 | 800 | 800 | 170 | 10 | 10 | 120 | 30 |
| Males | 50 | 1.3 | 1.5 | 17 | 1.7 | 150 | 2.0 | 1,200 | 1,200 | 270 | 12 | 15 | 150 | 40 |
| | 60 | 1.5 | 1.8 | 20 | 2.0 | 200 | 2.0 | 1,200 | 1,200 | 400 | 12 | 15 | 150 | 50 |
| | 60 | 1.5 | 1.7 | 19 | 2.0 | 200 | 2.0 | 1,200 | 1,200 | 350 | 10 | 15 | 150 | 70 |
| | 60 | 1.5 | 1.7 | 19 | 2.0 | 200 | 2.0 | 800 | 800 | 350 | 10 | 15 | 150 | 70 |
| | 60 | 1.2 | 1.4 | 15 | 2.0 | 200 | 2.0 | 800 | 800 | 350 | 10 | 15 | 150 | 70 |
| Females | 50 | 1.1 | 1.3 | 15 | 1.4 | 150 | 2.0 | 1,200 | 1,200 | 280 | 15 | 12 | 150 | 45 |
| | 60 | 1.1 | 1.3 | 15 | 1.5 | 180 | 2.0 | 1,200 | 1,200 | 300 | 15 | 12 | 150 | 50 |
| | 60 | 1.1 | 1.3 | 15 | 1.6 | 180 | 2.0 | 1,200 | 1,200 | 280 | 15 | 12 | 150 | 55 |
| | 60 | 1.1 | 1.3 | 15 | 1.6 | 180 | 2.0 | 800 | 800 | 280 | 15 | 12 | 150 | 55 |
| | 60 | 1.0 | 1.2 | 13 | 1.6 | 180 | 2.0 | 800 | 800 | 280 | 10 | 12 | 150 | 55 |
| Pregnant | 70 | 1.5 | 1.6 | 17 | 2.2 | 400 | 2.2 | 1,200 | 1,200 | 320 | 30 | 15 | 175 | 65 |
| Lactating | 95 | 1.6 | 1.8 | 20 | 2.1 | 280 | 2.6 | 1,200 | 1,200 | 355 | 15 | 19 | 200 | 75 |
| | 90 | 1.6 | 1.7 | 20 | 2.1 | 260 | 2.6 | 1,200 | 1,200 | 340 | 15 | 16 | 200 | 75 |

[c] Retinol equivalents. 1 retinol equivalent = 1 mg retinol or 6 mg b-carotene.
[d] As cholecalciferol. 10 mg cholecalciferol = 400 IU of vitamin D.
[e] a-Tocopherol equivalents. 1 mg d-a tocopherol = 1 a-TE.
[f] 1 NE (niacin equivalent) is equal to 1 mg of niacin or 60 mg of dietary tryptophan.

*Recommended Dietary Allowances*, © 1989 by the National Academy of Sciences, National Academy Press, Washington, DC.

## Sample Workout Schedule

| | Week No. | SUN | MON | TUE | WED | THU | FRI | SAT |
|---|---|---|---|---|---|---|---|---|
| Exercise<br>Minutes<br>Intensity Level | 1 | walk<br>15<br>65% | | walk<br>15<br>65% | | walk<br>15<br>65% | | walk<br>15<br>65% |
| Exercise<br>Minutes<br>Intensity Level | 2 | walk<br>15<br>65% | | walk<br>15<br>65% | | walk<br>15<br>65% | | walk<br>15<br>65% |
| Exercise<br>Minutes<br>Intensity Level | 3 | walk<br>20<br>65% | | walk<br>20<br>65% | | walk<br>20<br>65% | | walk<br>20<br>65% |
| Exercise<br>Minutes<br>Intensity Level | 4 | walk<br>20<br>65% | 10<br>sit-ups | walk<br>20<br>65% | | walk<br>20<br>65% | 10<br>sit-ups | walk<br>20<br>65% |
| Exercise<br>Minutes<br>Intensity Level | 5 | walk<br>20<br>70% | 11<br>sit-ups | walk<br>20<br>70% | 11<br>sit-ups | walk<br>20<br>70% | 11<br>sit-ups | walk<br>20<br>70% |
| Exercise<br>Minutes<br>Intensity Level | 6 | walk<br>20<br>70% | 12<br>sit-ups | walk<br>20<br>70% | 12<br>sit-ups | walk<br>20<br>70% | 12<br>sit-ups | walk<br>20<br>70% |
| Exercise<br>Minutes<br>Intensity Level | 7 | walk<br>25<br>70% | 13<br>sit-ups | walk<br>25<br>70% | 13<br>sit-ups | walk<br>25<br>70% | 13<br>sit-ups | walk<br>25<br>70% |
| Exercise<br>Minutes<br>Intensity Level | 8 | walk<br>30<br>70% | 14<br>sit-ups | walk<br>30<br>70% | 14<br>sit-ups | walk<br>30<br>70% | 14<br>sit-ups | walk<br>30<br>70% |

Maximum Heart Rate 220 − __36__ (age) = __184__ (or MAX)

Intensity level: __184__ (MAX) × 0.65 = __120__ at 65%

__184__ (MAX) × 0.70 = __129__ at 70%

__184__ (MAX) × 0.75 = __138__ at 75%

__184__ (MAX) × 0.80 = __147__ at 80%

## Sample Workout Schedule

| | Week No. | SUN | MON | TUE | WED | THU | FRI | SAT |
|---|---|---|---|---|---|---|---|---|
| Exercise<br>Minutes<br>Intensity Level | | | | | | | | |
| Exercise<br>Minutes<br>Intensity Level | | | | | | | | |
| Exercise<br>Minutes<br>Intensity Level | | | | | | | | |
| Exercise<br>Minutes<br>Intensity Level | | | | | | | | |
| Exercise<br>Minutes<br>Intensity Level | | | | | | | | |
| Exercise<br>Minutes<br>Intensity Level | | | | | | | | |
| Exercise<br>Minutes<br>Intensity Level | | | | | | | | |
| Exercise<br>Minutes<br>Intensity Level | | | | | | | | |

Maximum Heart Rate 220 − _____ (age) = _____ (or MAX)

Intensity level: _____ (MAX) × 0.65 = _____ at 65%

_____ (MAX) × 0.70 = _____ at 70%

_____ (MAX) × 0.75 = _____ at 75%

_____ (MAX) × 0.80 = _____ at 80%

# Bibliography

## Chapter 1

R. Jackson. *Doctors and Diseases in the Roman Empire*. Norman: University of Oklahoma Press, 1988.

N. Lewis. *Life in Egypt under Roman Rule*. Oxford, UK: Clarendon Press, 1985.

R. Schumacher, J. Klippel, and D. Robinson, eds. *Primer on Rheumatic Diseases*, 9th ed. Atlanta: Arthritis Foundation, 1988.

## Chapter 2

M. McGoldrick and R. Gerson. *Genograms in Family Assessment*. New York: W. W. Norton & Co., 1985.

R. Schumacher, J. Klippel, and D. Robinson, eds. *Primer on Rheumatic Diseases*, 9th ed. Atlanta: Arthritis Foundation, 1988.

# Chapter 3

R. I. Fox et al. "Potential Role of Epstein-Barr Virus in Sjogren's Syndrome." *Rheumatic Disease Clinics of North America* 13, no. 2 (August 1987).

L. Goodman and A. Gilman, eds. *The Pharmacological Basis of Therapeutics*, 5th ed. New York: Macmillan, 1970.

S. Kennedy-Stoskopf et al. "Lentivirus—Induces Arthritis." *Rheumatic Disease Clinics of North America* 13, no. 2 (August 1987).

R. Schumacher, J. Klippel, and D. Robinson, eds. *Primer on Rheumatic Diseases*, 9th ed. Atlanta: Arthritis Foundation, 1988.

C. Smith et al. "Parvoviruses: Infections and Arthropaties." *Rheumatic Disease Clinics of North America* 13, no. 2 (August 1987).

R. L. Wilder. "Proinflammatory Microbial Products as Etiologic Agents of Inflammatory Arthritis." *Rheumatic Disease Clinics of North America* 13, no. 2 (August 1987).

# Chapter 4

O. J. Clemmensen et al. "Psoriatic Arthritis Treated with Oral Zinc Sulphate." *British Journal of Dermatology* 103 (1980).

L. G. Darlington. "Does Food Intolerance Have Any Role in the Aetiology and Management of Rheumatoid Disease?" *Annals of Rheumatic Diseases* 44 (1985).

M. R. Eades. *Thin So Fast*. New York: Warner Books, 1989.

F. McCrae et al. "Diet and Arthritis." *The Practitioner* 230 (April 1986).

G. B. Moment. "Aging, Arthritis and Food Allergies: A Research Opportunity Revisited." *Growth* 44 (1980).

H. L. Newbold. *Mega-Nutrients: A Prescription for Total Health*. Los Angeles: The Body Press, 1987.

R. S. Panush et al. "Diet Therapy for Rheumatoid Arthritis." *Arthritis and Rheumatism* 26, no. 4 (April 1983).

*Recommended Dietary Allowances*, 9th ed. Washington, DC: National Academy Press, 1980.

D. R. Robinson. "Lipid Mediators of Inflammation." *Rheumatic Disease Clinics of North America* 13, no. 2 (August 1987).

P. G. Wolman. "Management of Patients Using Unproven Regimens for Arthritis." *Journal of the American Dietetic Association* 87, no. 9 (September 1987).

## Chapter 5

R. Cailliet and L. Gross. *The Rejuvenation Strategy*. New York: Doubleday, 1987.

M. R. Eades. *Thin So Fast*. New York: Warner Books, 1989.

## Chapter 6

E. Rubenstein and D. Federman. *Scientific American Medicine*. New York: Scientific American, 1988.

R. Schumacher, J. Klippel, and D. Robinson, eds. *Primer on Rheumatic Diseases*, 9th ed. Atlanta: Arthritis Foundation, 1988.

## Chapter 7

L. Goodman and A. Gilman, eds. *The Pharmacological Basis of Therapeutics*, 5th ed. New York: Macmillan, 1970.

R. Schumacher, J. Klippel, and D. Robinson, eds. *Primer on Rheumatic Diseases*, 9th ed. Atlanta: Arthritis Foundation, 1988.

## Chapter 8

S. R. Covey. *The Seven Habits of Highly Effective People*. New York: Simon & Schuster, 1989.

## Chapter 9

K. Lorig and J. F. Fries. *The Arthritis Helpbook*. Reading, MA: Addison-Wesley Publishing Co., 1988.

# Glossary

**Allele.** One member of a gene pair that occupies the same position on a specific chromosome and carries information about a specific trait.

**Anaphylaxis.** An immediate and potentially life-threatening allergic reaction brought about by extreme allergic sensitivity to a substance.

**Antibody.** An immune substance produced by the body in response to an antigen (foreign substance) and that reacts and binds specifically to that antigen.

**Antigen.** Any of various sorts of foreign proteins or foreign cells or tissues that induce a state of sensitivity in the body.

**Arthralgia.** Joint pain.

**Arthritis.** Inflammation of a joint or joints.

**Cartilage.** A resilient but firm connective or fibrous tissue that covers the ends of bones.

**Chromosome.** One member of twenty-three pairs of such structures (in humans) found in the nucleus of all the cells of the body that bear the genetic material.

**Dermatitis.** Any inflammation of the skin. Can be manifested as rashing, scaling, blistering, crusting, etc.

**Diarthrodal joint.** A hinge-type joint.

**Dominant trait.** A characteristic of inheritance strong enough that if either allele of a gene pair passes it along, it will always be expressed.

**Enzyme.** A protein secreted by cells that acts as a stimulator to induce chemical changes in other substances, but remains unchanged by the process.

**Gene.** The functional unit of heredity which consists of a discrete segment of the giant DNA molecule. Each gene pair codes for a specific body protein, the visible result of which is the characteristic traits that make us what we are.

**Gene expression.** The visible result of the work of the genes.

**Gene pool.** All the possible chromosomes, genes, or alleles coding for all possible traits in the human organism.

**Genome.** The complete set of chromosomes derived from one parent (twenty-three in humans) or the total gene complement of a set of chromosomes.

**Immunogenetics.** The branch of genetics concerned with inheritance of differences in antigens or antigenic responses.

**Mucin.** A protein-sugar substance found in connective tissue, joint fluid, and other glandular secretions.

**Pannus.** The mass of tissue that forms in the rheumatoid joint from the proliferation or excess growth of the joint lining or synovium.

**Recessive trait.** A characteristic inherited in the genes that requires passage by both members of the gene pair to result in its expression.

**Synovium.** The thin layer of tissue that lines a joint.

**Systemic.** Involving or pertaining to the body as a whole, to all the systems of the body.

**TENS.** An acronym standing for Transcutaneous Electrical Nerve Stimulator, which is a machine used in physical therapy to apply low-voltage electric current across the skin of a painful area to incite the body to produce endogenous opiates (its own natural narcotic substances) to control pain without drugs.

**Tophus.** A lump of urate crystals (uric acid) deposited in the skin near joints or in the ear or in bone in gouty arthritis.

**Trait (inherited).** A characteristic, especially one that distinguishes an individual from others.

# Index